NEW JERSEY
STATE TROOPERS, 1961–2011

NEW JERSEY
STATE TROOPERS, 1961–2011

SERGEANT FIRST CLASS (RETIRED)
JOHN E. O'ROURKE

THE
History
PRESS

Published by The History Press
Charleston, SC 29403
www.historypress.net

First published 2012

ISBN 978.1.60949.218.2

Library of Congress Cataloging-in-Publication Data

O'Rourke, John, 1962-
New Jersey state troopers, 1961-2011 : remembering the fallen / John E.
O'Rourke.
p. cm.
Includes bibliographical references.
ISBN 978-1-60949-218-2
1. New Jersey. Division of State Police--History. 2. Police--Mortality--New Jersey-
-Case studies. 3. Traffic fatalities--New Jersey--Case studies. 4. Police--Violence
against--New Jersey--Case studies. I. Title.
HV8145.N5O763 2012
363.2092'2749--dc23
2011049606

CONTENTS

CONTENTS

FOREWORD

I met John O'Rourke several years ago when he became my supervisor, my squad sergeant. I worked under his supervision for several years, and during this time, he and I had many conversations covering a wide range of topics. We learned about each other's likes and dislikes—me being a huge New York Mets fan and him being a fan of Elvis Presley were two of the most significant topics I can remember. Just as we learned about each other, the topic often arose about those troopers who had died in the line of duty. We often wondered what type of men they were—their family backgrounds, where they were born and raised and so on. Basically, it was a curiosity to see if we had things in common with the troopers from the old days.

Troopers always go to work recognizing the inherent danger of their chosen profession, but for those unfortunate few, this stark reality was realized. I firmly believe that it is of utmost importance to recognize and always remember those whose actions were integral in establishing—through their sacrifice—many of the virtues that govern the state police today. I hope that you, too, come away from this book with the belief that these men always deserve to be revered and honored.

The narratives you are about to read are profound and personal. Much research and care has been taken in order to present an accurate and proper depiction of the troopers contained in this book. I had the pleasure of teaching Trooper Castellano #6397 at a state police in-service. I graduated from the 117th State Police class with the son of Trooper Dawson #2141.

And I had the unfortunate luck of working the day Trooper Gonzalez was murdered. Sadly, I have attended the funerals of several troopers. These experiences have convinced me of the importance of telling these troopers' stories.

One of the unenviable duties of a trooper is attending funerals of the fallen. There are many aspects to these services that set them apart from traditional funerals, particularly the number of people in attendance, as well as the number of dignitaries, elected officials, troopers and officers from all parts of our country. But specifically for a trooper, other troopers from as near as New York and Pennsylvania to as far as California and Alaska come to pay their respects, as we do when one of theirs has fallen in the line of duty. The fact that troopers and officers from all parts come to show their support and pay their respects is touching and astonishing. The bond between members of law enforcement is far reaching and timeless. The size and scope of the contingent of participants is most impressive, especially when coupled with scores of the bagpipers, color guards and other assorted ceremonial units. The precision with which the legions of troopers move is a lesson in synchronization. These aspects are very impressive and captivating, even more so during such a time of sadness and bereavement. Notable is the sight of the casket, an imposing reminder of how close we all are to paying the ultimate sacrifice. But most significant of all is the sight of the families. The realization that the trooper was a husband, father, brother, uncle, relative or friend makes one reflect on one's own mortality.

It has been an honor being a part of this book, as well as the first volume, *Jersey Troopers: Sacrifice at the Altar of Public Service*. I am forever grateful to my sergeant and friend for including me in his undertaking. Who would have thought that he and I would take on such an arduous task and successfully see it through to the end? Much has occurred since the beginning of our journey. John is now retired and has moved on to his other professional endeavor. I have been promoted to the rank of sergeant, a position that requires me to ensure the safety of my subordinates—at times a very trying and difficult task. I hope you agree with me when I say that we represented the troopers in both books with the reverence, honor and respect that they have earned.

Sergeant Eliecer Ayala #5555

ACKNOWLEDGEMENTS

I would like to thank the following people for their help in making this book possible: Mazie Staas; Carol Lee Fiola; Louis Taranto; Agnes and Jacquelyn DeFrino; Thomas Bell; Joseph Broski; Patricia (Lukis) LeClair; Robert Kavula; Shela (Kavula) Carebellese; Joann Prato; Cheryl (Moesta) Storck; Christopher Moesta; Lynne (Segeren) Freedman; Ronald Perozzi; James Principe; Ronald Foster; Ingrid and Sean Dawson; Grace, Diane, Debbie and Donna Lamonaco; John Delesio; Dorothy and Brian McCarthy; Noreen (McCarthy) Cryan; Nona (McCarthy) Dalrymple; Clinton Pagano; Rita Errickson; Jennie and Daniel Negron; Michele Carroll; Christopher Carroll; Peggy Mallen; Nancy Moos; Nancy Hanratty; Carol, Frank, Raymond, Jeanne and Judy Bellaran; Patrick O'Dwyer; Maureen Gonzalez; Andrea Zimmerman; Denise Zimmerman; Donna (Castellano) Setaro; Stephanie Castellano; and Mark Falzini (NJSP archivist).

Thanks to the New Jersey State Police, Former Troopers Association, the Survivors of the Triangle and all of the local, county and state libraries that assisted in this research.

A special thanks to the countless others (too numerous to mention) for helping me with this book. I am grateful to all.

I would also like to thank Eliecer "El" Ayala for proofreading my manuscript and for all of his helpful suggestions. Lastly, thanks to my wife, Ann, and my two children, John and Joanna, for their support and encouragement.

SANDWICH AND A COFFEE

JOHN W. STAAS #1382

In the early to mid-1600s, European settlers began coming to the banks of the Delaware River to what today is Camden City. The fur trade was the catalyst for settlement in this area; later, Philadelphia's growth brought additional people, as Camden sits across the river. Philadelphia was the largest city in America, and ferries brought the two cities together. Over the course of the next century, Camden sat in the shadows of Philadelphia. However, when the nineteenth century beckoned, a Camden and Amboy railroad line was built that provided direct access to New York City. Now, Philadelphians were dependent on Camden to get to what was the largest metropolis, New York City. Throughout the Industrial Revolution, Camden flourished up until the first part of the twentieth century. Toward the end of this growth period, John Staas—the subject of this narrative—was born. The date was Friday, July 22, 1927.[1]

Staas's father, Richard, was Dutch German and a second-generation American who married Anna (née Knowles), also of Dutch German descent. Anna also had roots in Ireland and was part Native American. She was an attractive woman; with her dark features, high cheekbones and long black hair, she embodied her Native American roots. Richard and Anna lived in a modest home at 3424 Freemont Street and had four children: Richard, Emma, Calvin and John.[2]

Not much is known of John Staas's upbringing other than that he attended the public school in town and later Woodrow Wilson High School. During

Trooper John Staas. *Courtesy of Mazie Staas.*

his tenure in high school, Staas was an exceptional basketball player, an all-star during each of his four years of play. John also played football, but twenty years after he graduated, his basketball photo was still hanging in the trophy case at Woodrow Wilson High.[3]

After graduating, Staas enlisted in the United States Navy. At the age of eighteen, he stood six feet tall, had light-brown hair, a slender build and blue eyes and looked impressive in his white navy uniform. Staas entered the service near the end of World War II and spent his entire tour stateside as a cook. It is believed that during this period he met and married a woman named Loraine; the two had a daughter named Gail in October 1947.[4]

After the service, John Staas worked at the Pennsylvania Lawn Mower Company in Camden and then as a timekeeper for Kellett Aircraft at the Camden Airport. His marriage to Loraine dissolved which opened the door for him to meet Lillian Mae Granville.[5]

It was the summer of 1950, and Harry "Speed" Wilson, a friend of John's, set him up on a date with a young woman named Lillian. John and Mazie (his pet name for her) had their blind date with Wilson and his girlfriend. The foursome spent the entire day soaking in the sun at Olympia Lakes in Burlington County. Staas quickly fell in love with Mazie. The two dated for the next two years, going on many trips together to places like Washington,

D.C., and the Jersey Shore. In a touching ceremony on Saturday, November 14, 1953, the two exchanged wedding vows. A honeymoon followed at his wife's family home in Middletown, New York. This place is a secluded retreat, and with John being an avid deer hunter, they visited it often through the following years.[6]

During the early stages of their marriage, John and Mazie lived in the Canterberry apartments in Camden. They celebrated their first New Year's as a married couple. The year 1954 proved to be a pivotal one for the two. John's brother had asked him to tag along when he was going to take the state police test. As it turned out, John passed but his brother did not.[7]

Mazie and John celebrated their first wedding anniversary walking around the state police training facility, as John was still weeks away from graduating. That day came on Monday, December 20, 1954, with Trooper Staas receiving badge #1382. Interestingly, Girbert Pagano #1378—brother of Lester and Clinton Pagano—graduated on this date as well. For the Paganos, the state police was a family tradition. The tradition would become part of the Staas family, too.[8]

Trooper Staas's first two assignments came at the Malaga Barracks and then at Mays Landing. In September 1955, a son, Joseph Staas, was born to the couple. During this period, troopers were living in the barracks and spent long tours away from their families. Raising a child basically on her own, Mazie found it difficult, but the two worked through the difficulties of being a trooper. The couple managed to save enough money and purchased a gray three-bedroom ranch at 1013 West White Horse Pike in Cologne, New Jersey. Then, in April 1957, Mazie gave birth to Jackie Lyn. When Jackie was born, Staas was working out of the Hammonton Station. Their fifth wedding anniversary was celebrated with the birth of yet another son, whom they named after John. John and Mazie adored their children and spent countless hours with them. John loved kids and often played with the neighborhood children, who enjoyed his company and would come asking if he was around. Staas was a wonderful role model.[9]

Staas (right), with fellow a trooper. *Courtesy of Mazie Staas.*

John and Mazie were enjoying their life together and had a full house with three children and Gail spending the summers with her father. Gail became like a daughter to Mazie. Summers saw the Staas family heading up to Middletown. The children loved the large property, as did Dad—he hunted deer in the woods surrounding the property. At night, the couple would break out their ukuleles and play together; John played the banjo ukulele and Mazie the baritone. Many parties had the couple entertaining for family and friends. John's favorite song to play was "Ghost Riders in the Sky." Another hobby of his was bowling, and he belonged to a number of leagues.[10]

Meanwhile, Staas was earning the trust and respect of troopers, with many saying that he was a "capable and personable" person. Others said that he was a "pretty jolly sort of guy who was liked by everyone." Another said that Staas was "one of the better men in the department."[11]

By December 1961, Staas was thirty-four and a tenured trooper with six years under his Sam Brown. In the fall, he and Mazie celebrated their children's birthdays; Joseph turned six, Gail turned fourteen and John turned three. The years had quickly passed by.[12]

After Thanksgiving, the family began to look toward the upcoming Christmas season. On Friday, December 1, John Staas was working the midnight shift and was looking forward to the next day, as he was about to begin a week's vacation hunting. The bulk of his day would be hunting followed by warm nights with Mazie and the kids. On this particular Friday, it was slow, and John stopped home for dinner. Mazie said that John was in "good spirits," and she and the kids enjoyed a nice meal with him before he headed back to patrol.[13]

Hitting the road again, Trooper Staas assisted a motorist who had broken down and also attended court in Folsom. A few minutes before midnight, John stopped in at the Hammonton Barracks to work on reports. There, he, Trooper Michael Phillips #1590 and Sergeant Fred Brown #640 spoke for a while. Brown then went to bed and left the two troopers working on their pending reports. The two decided to get coffee and food, with Staas volunteering to pick it up.[14]

John Staas started troop car no. 215 and pulled out of the station lot and onto the White Horse Pike (Route 30). A fog thick as pea soup had set in over the area, and John found it difficult to see. While driving, he spotted a truck commit a violation and turned to pursue it. Upon moving closer to the truck, the fog's density made Staas misjudge his distance from the truck, and he struck it from behind. The impact caused him to

John Staas administering a drunkometer test. *Courtesy of Mazie Staas.*

lose control, striking a tree. In an instant, the life of John Staas had come to an end.[15]

Out of the silence of the night came a knock at the door. Mazie stumbled out of bed to answer it. Standing there were Lieutenant Jessie Souder #499 and Sergeant Brown. One of the most difficult things a trooper can do is tell a wife that her husband has been killed. However, the uncaring coldness of the words delivered on that horrible morning haunt Mazie to this day. "I said, 'How is he?'" Souder responded, "He isn't."[16]

A close friend and colleague, Trooper Bill Sahli #1347, stayed with her and the children until after the funeral, taking care of all of the arrangements. Trooper John Staas was buried at the Locustwood Cemetery off Route 70 in Erlton, New Jersey.[17]

Joseph Staas grew to be a young man who followed in his dad's footsteps. He enlisted in the state police on May 20, 1977, as a member of the ninety-second class. Colonel Clinton Pagano asked Mazie to present the badge to her son, marking the first time that a civilian had done so. Trooper Joseph Staas #3148 was presented with a nightstick by members of his father's class.[18]

By December, the seven-month tenured trooper was twenty-two years old and had a wife, two small daughters and a son. Ironically, on the anniversary of his dad's death, Joseph was working the midnight shift out of the Bridgton Station. It's safe to say that his father crossed his mind during the evening. In a sick twist of fate, on the way home from work, Joseph Staas fell asleep and veered off the road, striking a tree. Just like his father, his life ended in an instant.[19]

Heartache would come again to the Staas family when Gail was killed in an automobile accident at the same age her father was when he died. If there must be a postscript to this sad story, let it be a celebration of John Staas's four grandchildren and four great-grandchildren.[20]

IN-SERVICE TRAINING

RAYMOND P. FIOLA #1399

On a cold Christmas Eve in 1924, Philip Fiola and his wife, Anna, received an early present: a son they chose to name Raymond Philip. Philip Fiola was of Italian descent and, according to relatives, worked as a local police officer somewhere in the Bergen County area. Anna, of Czechoslovakian descent, was a housewife. The couple had moved to Wallington, Bergen County, New Jersey. General George Washington rode through this area and retreated across the Passaic River, near what today is Gregory Avenue. One hundred years before, the Leni-Lenape Indians hunted in and around what is now Wallington. Here in this community, the Fiolas raised their two children, Raymond and Clara.[21]

Their children attended grammar school and high school in Wallington. Raymond was your average young man both socially and academically. He and his sister grew up at a time in American history when everyone felt the constraints of the economy. The Great Depression, as it came to be known, played havoc on American families. Because the children did not have the luxury of toys, they used to play games such as kick the can and stickball. Despite their struggles, Philip and Anna never complained.[22]

While in high school, Raymond (or Ray, as his friends called him) was a member of the drum and bugler team. In typing class, he met Josephine Taranto. The two fired up a courtship that would endure to adulthood. During their high school tenure, world events cast a dark shadow across the globe. In their freshman year of 1940, all eyes were on Germany as it occupied Austria,

Trooper Raymond Fiola #1399. *Courtesy of the New Jersey State Police.*

an event that set into motion a chain of events that led to the Second World War. In the spring of 1941, the United States began strategic discussions for possible hostilities—thoughts of avoidance were no longer entertained. The attack on Pearl Harbor came two weeks before Ray Fiola's seventeenth birthday. Patriotic fervor filled the nation, and men all over the country began enlisting in the United States military. Fiola was no different. He, too, felt the calling, but at seventeen, he needed his parents' permission. The red-blooded American parents gave their blessing, and their son enlisted in the United States Marine Corps.[23]

During the war, Fiola had several furloughs in the beautiful and scenic Hawaii. It was a far cry from the topography of the Garden State. Raymond Fiola didn't talk much of his wartime exploits; when he did, it was with other men. He was an old-fashion man and believed that some things are best left unsaid.[24]

After his war service, Raymond and his high school sweetheart were married on Sunday, January 27, 1946. A brief honeymoon in New York City followed. Two months later, Josephine was pregnant. The twenty-one-year-old soon-to-be father worked many jobs to put food on the table. The couple moved to 842 Paterson Avenue in East Rutherford, New Jersey. Just as he was an early Christmas gift to his parents, so too was his daughter, Carol Lee, who was born on December 14. Needless to say, Christmas Eve 1946 was a special day for Ray and his beloved wife, Josephine.[25]

The year 1947 was welcomed with thoughts of a long, happy life together as they built their family. For the next nine years, that's just what they enjoyed. These years witnessed great domestic bliss as the two watched their daughter grow and become "Daddy's little girl." Ray continued in different companies, trying to find his niche, but he never failed to provide for his family.[26]

Josephine's little brother, Louis, was only about eleven when his older sister wed. To Louis, Ray was his role model. Ray often took Lou fishing.

Fiola loved his little brother-in-law and had high hopes for the young man. The relationship between the two set the stage for Louis' future—and the state police, for that matter.[27]

Fate had Raymond Fiola finding a vocation into which he could settle, the New Jersey State Police. Training began in January 1955 with seventy-six people, forty-seven of whom graduated as members of the forty-eighth class on Sunday, May 1, 1955. Trooper Raymond Fiola received badge #1399.

Significant changes were occurring in the "outfit" as these new troopers began patrol. Joseph D. Rutter was superintendent, and during his tenure, he moved the organization to a five-troop configuration, a system structure that is still in effect today: A, for south, B, for north, C, for central, D, for New Jersey Turnpike and E, for Garden State Parkway.[28]

Trooper Fiola was assigned to Troop C and began on Monday, May 2, 1955, under blue skies at the New Brunswick Station. His beginning months were not marked by any significant events. However, the year that followed forty-eighth's graduation was cruel to the organization, with John Anderson #1190 and George Dancy #1481 being killed in the line of duty.[29]

In September 1956, Fiola was transferred to the Riverton Station in rural Burlington County. Riverton is a beautiful community that gets its name from the sprawling Delaware River adjacent to the town. Fiola worked here until November 1956, when he was transferred to Holmdel Station. His first day there was Friday, November 16. The Holmdel Station was a brick facility that sat on the property of the arts center in Holmdel.[30]

In December, Ray and Josephine celebrated Carol Lee's tenth birthday and capped the year off with Ray's thirty-third birthday. The normal seasonal holiday events followed.[31]

In late January 1957, Fiola was transferred to the Pleasant Plains Station, which is located farther south on the parkway and sits on the median strip of the northbound and southbound lanes.[32]

The Pleasant Plains transfer put a toll on the Fiola family. The commute was long, and Ray found himself spending less and less time with Josephine and Carol Lee. So, the couple began looking at homes in and around the Toms River area. They found a quant family community in town known as the Indian Hill Estates. It was a new development in Toms River, and the streets were beautifully lined with trees. The address was 976 McGuire Drive. In January 1958, Josephine announced that she was with child. It had been nearly twelve years since their first was born. The two were ecstatic. On Monday, October 6, 1958, John Philip Fiola was born.[33]

Parade rest. *Courtesy of Carol Lee Fiola.*

The year 1958 witnessed the state police continuing to grow in responsibility, evolving from the rural police force conceived in 1921. In March, the "boots and breeches" dress code was discontinued. Troopers started wearing slacks and shoes. September saw the creation of the underwater recovery unit, which was the first of its kind among state police agencies. Lou Taranto followed in Fiola's footsteps and entered the Marine Corps. Afterward, he continued on the same path plowed by his brother-in-law and became a Jersey trooper as a member of the fifty-fourth class. Trooper Taranto #1594 rose to lieutenant colonel. That alone is a befitting tribute to the influence of Ray Fiola.[34]

Off duty, Ray and Josephine spent many hours in their yard with Carol Lee and John. It was a wonderful time, and they appreciated each moment. Time was moving fast; Carol Lee was growing into a woman, and John was soon walking.[35]

On October 22, 1959, Raymond Fiola was once again transferred, this time back to Troop C at the Toms River Station. It was a move that he presumably requested.[36]

The next two years saw Trooper Fiola patrolling out of Toms River. Little has been preserved of his activities during his tenure here. We move ahead to a cold day in February.

Monday, February 19, 1962, was a typically cold February day in the state of New Jersey. Ray had in-service training at Division Headquarters and headed out of the station with Trooper Stanley Adams #1316. Adams drove, selecting a brand-new 1962 state police Ford for their trek. The trip took the two men through rural communities in the central Jersey region. The weather and road conditions were poor on County Route 526 in Millstone, the blowing wind turning sections of the road to "black ice." Making matters worse was the falling snow. When Adams observed a school bus picking up children, he braked, and his vehicle slid on the icy road. Unable to maintain control of his car, he slid off the road into a ditch lined with trees.[37]

Raymond Fiola was rushed to Farmer's Hospital and was pronounced dead by Dr. Farmer. The impact into the trees caused massive bleeding in Fiola's heart.[38]

With full state police honors, Trooper Raymond Fiola was laid to rest at the Saint Joseph's Church Cemetery in Toms River.[39]

A DAY LIKE NO OTHER

Joseph P. DeFrino #1605

Anthony DeFrino and his wife, Agnes (née Adamo), were second-generation Italian Americans who took up residence in the small community of Lyndhurst, New Jersey. Anthony worked as an organ repairman and, later, as an electrician. Agnes worked sporadically as a seamstress. For a time, Anthony was without work and took advantage of this period by building their home at 707 Seventh Street—a red brick two-family house with white stucco. Once built, the DeFrinos rented the upstairs apartment to bring in a steady source of revenue. Anthony and Agnes's marriage bore three children: Joseph Paul on October 7, 1936; Marie Elaine in August 1942; and Jacquelyn in October 1945. Their first child is the subject of this narrative.[40]

Joseph DeFrino was a loving child who was very respectful and easy to care for. During his first six years of life, he was the only child. Thereafter, he was the only son. There was a bond between him and his mother that was much different than that of his sisters. Not a greater love, per se, but rather a bond that only a mother and son could have. He was the "light of his mother's eye." Joey, as he was called, entered school when world events were fixated on the hostile activities of World War II, but for little Joey DeFrino, he was having fun in school. Never one for serious academic study, he began at an early age to show that his attributes were social in nature. It seemed that everyone liked the little kid. He never seemed to find it difficult to make friends while at the Washington grammar school in Lyndhurst.[41]

By the time Joey DeFrino became a teenager, he had become very athletic and concerned with staying in shape and eating healthy. At Lyndhurst High, DeFrino also began to show an interest in working with his hands and in becoming a mechanic. Being a teenager in the 1950s was advantageous for an automobile enthusiast. Car manufacturers were building cars to attract the younger motorist, and Joey DeFrino was such a creator. This period is highlighted in the popular TV Series *Happy Days*, with kids driving up in their "hotrods" to sweet shops and listening to popular tunes on the jukebox. It was a wonderful time for a teenager in American history, and DeFrino enjoyed every moment of it. It was a common sight to see a shirtless DeFrino in his driveway working on a car. Hours upon hours were spent by him this way, recalled his sister Jackie. A particular memory of hers is of a hotrod that he had with a milk crate for a passenger seat. Joey would take her for rides, with her sitting dangerously on the box. Jackie has fond memories of her big brother. Laughing, she stated that one of them was him "putting me in the trunk and driving me around."[42]

Mom, Maria, Jacquelyn and Joseph. *Courtesy of Jacquelyn (DeFrino) Lynch.*

As DeFrino neared his eighteenth birthday, he stood six feet tall and weighed a lean 180 pounds. As he stood in his driveway with his black hair, brown eyes and muscular physique, he often caught the attention of girls walking by. As a teenager, Joey stayed away from popular teenage habits such as smoking, drinking and drug use. He lived a "clean" lifestyle and wanted to make the most out of his future. With an interest in mechanics, DeFrino enlisted in the United States Air Force.[43]

As DeFrino entered the air force, it was embarking on the first tests for jet-powered transportation of the newly built Boeing 707. It was a fascinating time in aviation history, as jet engines were going to be the next wave in transportation. For his part, DeFrino served as a mechanic and helped to ensure that these "birds" were safe and stayed in the air. His assignment was with the Eighth Fighter Bomber Squadron, and during his tenure there, his performance was recognized several times, most notably when he received "Airman of the Month." Four years were served by the Lyndhurst native before being honorably discharged. During these years, DeFrino was stationed overseas, with one tour being in Okinawa, Japan. With the service behind him, DeFrino moved back home to Seventh Street, where he began his next leg of life's journey.[44]

During the next year, the twenty-two-year-old mechanic tried to find his way in life. Then, in 1958, DeFrino took the written examination to be a state trooper. He applied for the fifty-fifth class and was accepted into that training academy. Trooper DeFrino #1605 was stationed at the Blairstown Station in Troop B; however, little else is known of his Troop B tours. In fact, this may have been his only assignment before his transfer to Troop D, working out of the Newark Station.[45]

On Easter Sunday 1962, Joey DeFrino asked Patricia Zilly, a twenty-year-old beauty from Red Bank, New Jersey, to marry him. The young couple set the date for October 20, 1962.[46]

Working on the turnpike is a challenging position for troopers. The turnpike is rich in state police history, but at the time of DeFrino's tenure, the road was less than a decade old. In that short time, however, Troopers Frank Trainor #682 and Hilary Welenc #1190 lost their lives patrolling it.[47]

In the forty-one years that had passed since the forming of the outfit, no year hit as hard as 1962. In February, Trooper Raymond Fiola #1399 was killed on duty, and then came the events of June 11, 1962.[48]

It was a hot June day with a bright blue sky above the turnpike and clear views of the Manhattan skyline. Troopers Arthur Abagnale #1671 and Milan Simcak #999 were working the day shift out of the Newark Station

Right: Joseph DeFrino. *Courtesy of Jacquelyn (DeFrino) Lynch.*

Below: Joking around. *Courtesy of Jacquelyn (DeFrino) Lynch.*

and, at the end of their tour, were being driven up to Interchange 18 in Secaucus by Trooper DeFrino. Today, the northern part of the turnpike has two roadways, an Eastern Extension and a Western Extension, but in 1962, the Western Extension had not been built yet. While traveling north on what is today the Eastern Extension, the three men in blue came upon a disabled truck in the right lane on the Passaic River Bridge. The exact location was milepost 108. They driver of the vehicle had been outside checking a flat. The troopers instructed him to drive his vehicle farther north to where there was a wide shoulder. While driving behind the truck, a commercial bus that was seventeen years old and had bad brakes came quickly upon them. The driver couldn't stop in time and literally drove the bus over the troop car, killing all three troopers.[49]

Jacquelyn DeFrino was ironing clothes when the phone rang. It was her aunt telling her of an accident in which Joey might have been involved. Moments later, the sad news was validated by a knock on the door.[50]

The impact of DeFrino's death was devastating. Joseph DeFrino predeceased everyone in his family, including his grandparents. His loss is still felt today by his loving mother, who is now in her nineties. Jacquelyn remembers just before her brother died how the three siblings had gone out on a triple date. It was a lovely evening and was the first time she had enjoyed an "adult" outing with her brother. This was going to be the first of many such occasions. However, this was not to be. Joseph DeFrino was buried at the Holy Cross Cemetery in North Arlington, New Jersey, in a somber service attended by hundreds of mourners.[51]

Milan Simcak #999

Milan Simcak had an interesting name, quite unusual among those listed on the rolls of dying in the line of duty. Simcak's heritage is partially of English descent, and his first name bears this out. Although the origin of the name "Milan" is from the province of Milan in Italy, it is a common name used by people of English descent. The surname of "Simcak" is of Slovakian origins. His parents lived in the city of Passaic, and there Milan was born on January 28, 1926.[52]

The first recorded information we have on Milan Simcak is his entry into the United States Army during World War II, during which he served at Headquarters Base M, rising to the rank of corporal. His service record from there is unclear, but he was given an honorable discharge. Employment history for Simcak is not known, and he disappears from history until his appointment to the thirty-eighth class for the state police.[53]

On December 18, 1950, the last three-digit badge number for the state police was issued to Trooper Milan Simcak upon his graduation. The twenty-four-year-old trooper was assigned to the northern part of the state, where he worked myriad assignments before his attachment to the New Jersey Turnpike. During his first year, Simcak's classmate, Trooper Emil Bock #974, was killed on duty. Then, in August 1951, Stanley Conn Jr. #947 died in an on-duty

Milan Simcak. *Courtesy of the New Jersey State Police.*

motorcycle accident. These were stark reminders of the dangers that he faced as a trooper.[54]

Sometime between 1954 and 1955, Simcak married a woman named Dorothy. The couple had two small children, David and Susan. Dorothy and Milan selected an up-and-coming area to raise their children: Paramus, New Jersey. Today, Paramus is known as a large community, with shopping malls attended by thousands of people daily. However, in the late 1950s, Paramus was nothing but farmland. Speculators realized that the farming markets were starting to die down and that the open space could be used for shopping centers and residential needs, as Paramus was located close to many major highways and New York City. This brought massive development to the area around the time of the Simcaks' residence here. Foremost in this development was the storefront. The Bergen Mall was built in 1952 and the Garden State Plaza in 1956. As a result of this development plan, the community went from fewer than ten thousand residents to more than twenty thousand in one year. Milan and Dorothy carved out a little parcel for themselves at 313 Spencer Place.[55]

At the time of Simcak's tenure, the turnpike and the parkway merged into Troop D. In all, Trooper Simcak served nearly twelve years as a trooper until that dreadful June day in 1962.[56]

Arthur J. Abagnale Jr. #1671

Arthur J. Abagnale Jr. was born in the Bronx, New York, on March 23, 1936. He was raised in New Jersey, where he attended grammar school at the Saint Anastasia School in Teaneck, New Jersey, and Oakland Military Academy in Oakland, New Jersey. Apparently, his family moved quite frequently, as his adolescent years were filled with attendance at a number of schools. He completed his grammar school education in Palisades Park at its Central Boulevard School.[57]

Apparently, a family move occurred in his teenage years, as well, as Abagnale went to high school in Leonia, which is in Bergen County. Arthur only attended three years of high school and enlisted in the United States Marine Corps when he was of age. While serving as a marine, Abagnale earned his high school diploma. As an adult, Arthur Abagnale Jr. was of average size, with dark skin and eyes and spoke fluent Italian—his dialect took on what was described as "Neapolitan" tones. Abagnale's service within the elite military organization ended with an honorable discharge.[58]

After his service, Abagnale attended night classes at the Hackensack High School for college credits in English and American history. While doing this, he decided to try his luck with the New Jersey State Police. After going through the various testing processes, the twenty-four-year-old entered the academy on Sunday, October 16, 1960. He endured sixteen weeks of grueling training before graduating on Monday, February 6, 1961. The fifty-fifth class had fifty-seven graduates (half had dropped out), with Arthur J. Abagnale Jr. receiving badge #1671.[59]

By the time of Abagnale's death in June 1962, his mother was deceased and his father was living in Cliffside Park, New Jersey, leaving the presumption that his mother had passed away years prior. Trooper Abagnale had moved out of his father's house and taken up residence on his own at 903 Elm Avenue in Ridgefield, a small community in Bergen County not far from where his father was living.

Trooper Arthur J. Abagnale Jr. #1671.
Courtesy of the New Jersey State Police.

Whether Abagnale was living alone cannot be determined, but it is believed that he was not in a serious relationship, as the local newspaper accounts recording his death and the subsequent investigations did not mention a significant other. Within the organization, Abagnale worked out of only two stations before his transfer to the Newark Station. The state police journey of Arthur Abagnale lasted only fourteen months and ended in what is still the most tragic day in state police history.[60]

Arthur J. Abagnale Jr.'s funeral took place on June 16 at the Blackley Funeral Home in Ridgefield, New Jersey. He was laid to rest at the Mount Carmel Cemetery in Tenafly, New Jersey.[61]

"SPIKE"

ANTHONY LUKIS JR. #1754

Patricia Imhoff was a fresh-faced kid who spent her adolescent years growing up in Beverly, which is near Burlington, New Jersey. Her parents, Raymond and Lillian (née McCardle), were of Irish German descent. Their little girl grew to be a beautiful teenager. She had long brown hair, hazel eyes and a slender build. She often turned boys' heads as she walked down the high school corridors. However, one day, there was a turn of events. A tall boy walking by her made her turn her head. "Just seeing him," she thought, "wow…he was a good-looking man [with] beautiful blue eyes." The boy's name was Anthony.[62]

Anthony Lukis Jr. was born on Wednesday, April 29, 1936, to Anthony and Maria (née Boyle). His father's family came from the republic of Lithuania in northern Europe. Lithuania is part of the three Baltic States and sits on the shore of the Baltic Sea. His mother, Maria, was of Irish heritage, and it is said that the Boyle surname comes from the Gaelic name "O Baoighill," which is supposedly derived from the Irish word *baigell*, meaning "having profitable pledges." The oldest-known Boyle family member was found in the county of Donegal, which is in the northernmost part of Ireland.[63]

The Lukises lived a modest life, with Anthony working as a factory worker at the Roebling Steel Mill in Roebling, New Jersey. John A Roebling had helped to develop the town, designing comfortable homes for his factory employees. The factory was responsible for building the Brooklyn Bridge.

Kim and her dad. *Courtesy of Patricia (Lukis) LeClair.*

Today, the mill is a museum, and the town has grown to more than eight thousand residents. When Anthony and Maria married, they moved in with her parents, John and Bertha. The Boyles were wonderful people, and Maria and Anthony treasured living there.[64]

By 1942, the couple had purchased a home of their own, a three-bedroom duplex at 320 Elm Avenue, a section of Burlington known as Farneville.

While Anthony worked at the mill, Maria stayed home as their family grew. In the fall of 1942, another son, Jack, was born. Then, two more sons followed: Paul in 1945 and Harold in 1950.[65]

Anthony Lukis Jr.—or "Spike," as Pat called him (friends called him Tony)—attended the Samuel Smith Grammar School, which was located on Elm Avenue. Afterward, he attended the Robert Stacey Grade School and then the Wilbur Watts High School. While in grade school, Lukis played football. In high school, he turned the ball in for a trumpet and played in the school band. "He was a great trumpet player," said Pat. The teenagers attended many high school events, with at least two outings per week. There was always something going on in the Burlington community. Every Wednesday night, a firehouse dance was attended by Spike and his future wife. Lukis would often say that he looked like Hollywood legend Richard Widmark, but Pat laughed and said, "Richard Widmark was a good-looking man, but my husband was better looking." Lukis was a man who had an air of confidence about him—at times "an attitude," Pat remembered. He was "very confident." The two dated for Lukis's senior year at Wilbur Watts.[66]

Upon graduating, Lukis worked as a bricklayer, putting in long, laborious hours. In 1956, he asked Pat to marry him. Soon, he grew tired of being a bricklayer and enlisted in the Marine Corps. He and Pat had discussed this transition, and she gave her blessing.[67]

Training for the young marine began at Parris Island; afterward, Lukis became an amphibious tank operator. These are the vessels that are commonly seen in war movies; they can operate as a boat and also drive up onto the shore. Upon completing his amphibious tank duties, Lukis was sent to Port Smith in New Hampshire and assigned as a military police officer. This position is credited with inspiring Lukis's later desire to enter law enforcement.[68]

Two days before turning eighteen, Pat and Spike married. The ceremony took place on Saturday, July 6, 1957, at Saint Paul's Roman Catholic Church in Burlington. Pat converted from her Presbyterian faith to Catholicism for her marriage. A reception followed at the local VFW Hall. Nearly 120 people were in attendance. The joyous night was followed by a honeymoon in a quaint cottage at Long Beach Island in a section of that town called Ship Bottom.[69]

In September, Lukis rented an apartment in Kittery, Maine, not far from the Portsmouth Military Base, with Pat moving up from New Jersey. In May 1958, Pat became pregnant and had to move back in with her parents. In July, their daughter, Kim Marie, was born. Spike was not there to see the birth of

Wedding day. *Courtesy of Patricia (Lukis) LeClair.*

his child, as his military service did not allow him leave. Sadly, in September, Grandpa Boyle died, leaving Grandma Boyle alone and vulnerable. Sadly, Grandma Boyle was sexually assaulted by a local deviant. As a result, she moved in with Anthony's mother, Maria.[70]

In January 1959, Lukis was honorably discharged and began working with the Brick Layers Union once again. In March, he, Pat and Grandma

Boyle moved into an apartment together on Lincoln Avenue in Farneville. Old Grandma Boyle was a strong Irish woman and bravely moved on after her assault. She helped raise Anthony until he was six years old. Lukis was the apple of her eye.[71]

Several state police tests were taken by Lukis, but he failed each one. It was the mathematical portion of the examination that he couldn't get by. In order to pass the test, Lukis was tutored in math. During this point in time, he and Pat were blessed with the birth of a son, Paul, on Saturday, March 19, 1960. In 1961, his math lessons paid off. "I got the notice and drove in the car to tell him at his job," said Pat. The two of them were so excited. The rest of the year witnessed Lukis proceeding through the selection process. When he entered the training academy, Pat was pregnant, and little money was in their pockets. Grandma Boyle's caring heart shown through once again, and she gave money so that they could buy their children Christmas presents.[72]

On Saturday, February 5, 1962, Lukis graduated as a member of the fifty-ninth class and received badge #1754. He was assigned to Troop A.[73]

It was a rough introduction for the young trooper, who was working out of the Woodstown Station. An uplifting moment for Lukis came on Friday, March 30, 1962, with the birth of a son, Michael. He and Pat tried to get a loan to purchase a home but were turned down by the bank. Troopers didn't make a lot of money during this period, and the Lukises were finding out the sacrifice that troopers make on a daily basis. Tony's parents loaned the couple the money to buy a home, and in March 1964, they purchased a three-bedroom, one-bath duplex at 128 Juniper Street in Burlington. Grandma Boyle moved in with them, and another son (Anthony III) was born to the couple in August 1964.[74]

At the age of twenty-eight, Tony and Pat had a large family and a roof over their heads. Lukis loved his family but was "private about his work." According to Pat, he "never said much about" being a trooper. Although money was tight, Spike and Pat liked to vacation at Long Beach Island. Pat liked to relax on the beach, while her husband enjoyed surfing and deep-sea fishing. Pat warmly remembered that "Spike was a good family man who loved his family and was a quiet person; just a good man." More than anything else, Tony was a devoted husband and father who "was very good with his children." The times spent together are cherished memories.[75]

"I was very proud of him," said Pat while speaking of her husband's vocation. And Lukis himself was proud of his accomplishments. He treasured his job and polished his gear and his hat badge on a regular basis. After his Woodstown assignment, Lukis was moved to the Red Lion Station, where he worked for a few years before being assigned to Troop D—an assignment that worried Pat, who was pregnant with their fifth child.[76]

Monday, June 7, 1965, was Lukis's first day on the superhighway. He was assigned to Moorestown Station, which patrols the southern portion of the highway.[77]

In January 1966, Pat gave birth to a daughter, Lana. Their family was complete, and this would be the last child for the couple. On May 3, 1966, the last page in the narrative of Anthony Lukis Jr. was written. It begins with Tony standing at the door of his home. "Why don't you call in sick?" Pat remembers asking him before he left to go to work. Lukis was feeling under the weather but was a dedicated trooper. He wanted to go in, and so he kissed his wife goodbye.[78]

In the early morning hours of Wednesday, May 4, Lukis observed a bronze Mustang with New York registration stopped on the shoulder at milepost 44.3. The man behind the wheel was fast asleep. His name was Daniel Connors Kremens—a resident of Brooklyn—and he was in possession of two loaded handguns. Trooper Lukis knocked on the window and startled Kremens. Lukis asked for the man's license and registration, and Kremens gave the trooper his license and told him that the registration was in the glove box. Daniel Kremens explains what happened next:

I was coming back from Virginia going towards home, and I was on the Turnpike. I got tired and pulled over. I locked the doors up, and shut the windows, and went to sleep. I left the dim lights on. I don't know how long I was sleeping when the officer woke me up. He asked me for my driver's license and registration. I gave him my license and the registration was in the glove compartment. I opened up the glove compartment, and the officer seen a bag in there. He asked me if it was whiskey. I told him, no. So, he asked me what it was, so I opened it up and showed him. It was two boxes of shells. He asked me if I had a gun in the car for the shells. I told him, no. Then he asked me what was in the other bag, and I gave the bag to him. I told him when I gave it to him that it was a twenty five automatic. He told me to get into his car. I got in, and I told him I gotta get my keys from my car. He said alright, so I got out, and went back to the car. At the same time, I picked up the thirty-two that I had in the car. I got out, and he told me to get back in the car. When I was sitting in the car, I asked him, "are you going to run me in for this?" Then he asked me, "Have you got the other gun

Kim, Dad and Paul. *Courtesy of Patricia (Lukis) LeClair.*

in the car for these other shells?" And I told him, no. He asked me, "What you got it on you?" I told him "Yes" and I gave him the gun. He told me to get out of the car, and I got out of the car. He told me to come around to the other side, and he was going to hand-cuff me. In the mean while he put the thirty two I gave him in his pocket. Then we got arguing there about him wanting to hand-cuff me and I didn't want to be hand-cuffed. I told him I would go with him without them. He kept on insisting, and I kept on insisting not to. Then he said he was going to call re-inforcements. He reached for the thing on the dash board, the speaker. When he did that, I rushed and I grabbed his arm. The next minute we were wrestling all over the ground. Then I heard a shot, and he went down, and I had the gun in my hand, and I shot him again. I panicked, and jumped in my car.[79]

Trooper Lukis was shot six times in the backside, two of which were to the head. The investigation revealed that three of these were fired within three inches of Lukis's body. Kremens's account is supported by a truck driver who witnessed the "tussling."[80]

Troopers Dory Saul #2004 and Barry Townsend #1915 spotted Kremens's Mustang a short distance from the crime, and a pursuit was initiated that lasted a nail-biting ten minutes. Subsequently, Kremens ran on foot and was found crouched under a porch step with two loaded guns in his possession, one of which was the murder weapon.[81]

Daniel Connors Kremens was sentenced to death, but in 1972, the death penalty was abolished, and his sentence was converted to life. Sent to a medium-security prison, he escaped in 1973. After sixteen days on the run, the state police learned that Kremens was in New York City. A tipster told Jersey Troopers that Kremens was about to purchase a gun in Times Square. Shortly after midnight on November 19, 1973, New Jersey State Police detective Sergeant Andrew Andaloro #1875, along with three New York City detectives, spotted Kremens on Fortieth Street near Eighth Avenue. As the lawmen approached, Kremens punched one officer and reached as if he was going for a weapon while putting his car into drive. Sergeant Andaloro fired three rounds into the back window of the car, ending the life of Daniel Kremens.[82]

Hearing of Kremens's death brought back memories of the May night when Pat had asked her husband to stay home. Later that night, she was awoken by a terrible banging on the door. "I looked out the window and saw the two troop cars," Pat said. "Our priest was with them." The sound of a knock at the door haunts her to this day. Pat has since installed a doorbell.[83]

SPILLED LOAD

THOMAS W. KAVULA #1809

Thomas's grandparents were Jozef and Mary Kavula, born and raised in Central Europe in the land now known as Slovakia, near the Russian border. Jozef was from a large family, as was his wife, Mary (née Simms). Jozef was not the oldest, so he was not in line to inherit the family farm, so he and Mary immigrated to America through Ellis Island. They settled in the Slovakian section of Bayonne, New Jersey. Bayonne provided ample employment and was primarily a blue-collar town, with dockworkers, candle makers, shoemakers and merchants. Here Jozef Kavula worked for Standard Oil. Seven children were born to the couple: John, Michael, Franz, Jozef, George, Mary and another child who died in infancy.[84]

Jozef and Mary's son Franz—or Frank, as he became known—had a close friend named David Smolen who had a younger sister with whom Frank would fall in love. In 1926, Frank graduated grammar school and began working for the Tidewater Oil Company.[85]

After the Great Depression, the twenty-one-year-old Frank opened up a tavern in the city, becoming the youngest tavern owner in the state. On Thanksgiving Day 1935, Ethel Smolen and Frank married in a ceremony at the Saint Joseph's Church on Avenue E. Interestingly, Ethel's grandparents were also named Jozef and Mary (née Knapp) and came from the same region of Slovakia as her husband's. In addition to owning the tavern, Frank worked as a building superintendent at the Bayonne Navy Base.[86]

Signing for the Cincinnati Reds as his father (right) looks on. *Courtesy of Robert Kavula.*

On Wednesday, May 25, 1938, the couple had their first child, a boy they named Robert. Three years later, in November 1941, the two were expecting their second child. World events were focused on the ongoing war, and tensions were building between Japan and America. Germany was on the offensive, and Hitler was becoming more powerful. In the midst of all this, the quiet Kavula household was filled with excitement and joy. Robert was getting bigger, and Frank and Ethel were preparing for the birth of their next child. That day came on Tuesday, November 4, 1941, with the birth of Thomas William Kavula.[87]

Thomas Kavula was christened on Sunday, December 7, as Pearl Harbor was being attacked. The couple tried to enjoy the celebrations but were closely monitoring events on the radio.[88]

The next several years witnessed the Kavulas moving to different locations in Bayonne. Then, in 1946, the couple purchased a vacant lot at 616 Broadway. There they built a restaurant that they proudly named Frank's Bar and Grill; there was an apartment upstairs.[89]

Frank's Bar and Grill became a popular place for lunch and dinner, and Frank had hoped that one day Robert and Thomas could take over the family business. The Kavulas were devout Catholics and attended church at Saint Joseph's on Avenue E, where the mass was given in Slovakian.[90]

Thomas grew to become a natural athlete and enjoyed organized sports. From an early age, he played baseball for the local Little League team, as well as the Babe Ruth League. Thomas's father was friends with Leo Paquin, who played football with Vince Lombardi and was part of the "Seven Blocks of Granite." Through this relationship, Frank was able to enroll Thomas in Xavier High School in New York City. Paquin, who was a teacher there, recruited Thomas to his baseball team.[91]

At an early age, Tom Kavula demonstrated an athletic ability far beyond others. Kavula's success at Xavier led to scholarships from Boston College, among others. However, the young man wanted to remain close to home and chose a basketball scholarship at Saint Peter's College in Jersey City.[92]

The Yankee farm team recruited Kavula, and for a time he wore the Yankee uniform and even practiced at Yankee Stadium. Then a scout for the Cincinnati Baseball Organization spotted Kavula on the field and invited him in early 1961 for a tryout. He was drafted to the Cincinnati Reds and occupied the roster along with Pete Rose. A slide into second base by Kavula resulted in a groin injury that took him off the team. In 1962, he was recruited to the Los Angeles Angels but soon lost his spot when his injury flared up again.[93]

While this was going on, Tom met a young Irish girl for whom he fell head over heels. This chance encounter happened in Jersey City when his aunt spotted a girl she thought was perfect for her nephew.[94]

Sheila O'Neil and Tom Kavula were seen all over town together. One of their favorite places was the CYO (Christian Youth Organization) in Jersey City. The CYO was a "happening place." Upstairs, people could roller-skate, while downstairs there was a bowling alley and an ice cream parlor. On Fridays, there was a dance. Admission was a whopping twenty cents. When not there, they hung out with friends; Sheila and Tom were both social by nature and spent many hours in the company of others.[95]

By New Year's Eve 1963, Thomas was entertaining thoughts of marriage. In early 1963, Kavula applied to the New Jersey State Police because he "wanted to be a trooper."[96]

On Saturday, February 2, 1963, Sheila and Tom were married at Saint Aden Church in Jersey City. It was bitterly cold, with a constant snowfall, and when Sheila arrived for the reception at Saint Joseph's School Hall, her gorgeous dress had been soiled black from the snow and dirt. A honeymoon was spent by the two at Mount Airy Lodge in the Pocono Mountains of Pennsylvania.[97]

At the time, Tom was working in the tavern, while his brother, Robert, was serving in the military. Having Tom in the tavern made his father happy. However, the state police would soon place Tom Kavula among its ranks.[98]

On Friday, March 17, 1963, Kavula's Irish wife, Sheila, celebrate Saint Patrick's Day on her own as her husband began his first day of academy training. Thirty-nine men began that day, with only sixteen eventually graduating as members of the sixty-first class. On Monday, June 10, 1963, Trooper Kavula #1809 formally entered the rolls of the outfit.[99]

In February 1964, the young couple celebrated their first anniversary with the joyful anticipation of their first child. Four days later, Karen Kavula was born.[100]

State files record little of Kavula's career, but his trooper experiences live on through stories he told his wife and brother. One such story involves an enraged farmer with a double-barreled shotgun. Told to Sheila nonchalantly over breakfast, Kavula had been working in the Clinton area when the call came in. Arriving Trooper Kavula was confronted by the man wielding the gun. The crazed and irate man had both barrels pointed at the young trooper. While negotiating with the man, Kavula was able to get close enough to wrestle the gun away. Tom told Sheila that he "hit the man as hard as he could."[101]

Trooper Thomas Kavula #1809. *Courtesy of the New Jersey State Police.*

Five years passed since his graduation day, and Tom Kavula was now patrolling the New Jersey Turnpike, working out of the Newark Station at Interchange 14.[102]

Robert remembered his brother taking him out on patrol one night. Bob was a commercial airline pilot and was on a layover; Tom wanted him to get a taste of what it was like to be a trooper. It was fascinating for Bob, and it made him realize the dangers that his little brother was facing on a daily basis.[103]

During this time in Kavula's tenure, the civil rights movement was taking place, and major cities throughout the country were experiencing civil unrest. Riots occurred in more than 125 cities throughout the country, with Newark and Jersey City being among them. Trooper Kavula had taken part in the Jersey City deployment to quell the unrest.[104]

Kavula had moved his family to 39 East Twenty-eighth Street in Bayonne, and his commute to Newark was short. His family life was of the utmost importance to him, and he and Sheila were enjoying raising Karen.[105]

On the morning of Thursday, September 19, 1968, Tom and Sheila awoke and had breakfast together along with little Karen. They discussed plans for later in the day and had decided to go to the park because the weather was going to be nice. As he walked out the door, he kissed his wife goodbye and went off to work.[106]

At about 8:30 a.m., a call came over his radio about a tractor trailer spill at Interchange 13 in Elizabeth. Kavula pulled up to the scene and observed that the spill had caused traffic congestion. At this location, workers had been constructing a ramp, and the turnpike authority had a temporary ramp leading toward the Goathals Bridge. Kavula stepped out of his troop car and began directing traffic.[107]

Harold L. Brower of Larwill, Indiana, was driving his International tractor-trailer and was directed by the trooper to proceed onto the Goathals Bridge ramp. As Brower cut his wheels, he did so too sharply, and his trailer knocked Kavula to the ground. The right rear tandem wheels of the trailer ran the young trooper over. After doing so, Brower failed to stop and continued toward the bridge. A concerned citizen named Joseph G. Taeffner of Monmouth Junction, New Jersey, hopped into Kavula's troop car and stopped the truck by the entrance of the bridge.[108]

Trooper Kavula was rushed to Elizabeth Hospital. "The only marks on his body [were] a compound fracture of a lower leg. The autopsy found a ruptured spleen. It took several hours for Trooper Kavula to bleed to death." Sadly, he passed away after much suffering. To this day, family members question the care that he received at the hospital.[109]

Harold Brower was arrested and charged with a variety of indictments, with the most serious being death by auto. On May 13, 1970, Brower was found not guilty of all charges, partially due to a haphazard state police investigation. The State of New Jersey appealed this verdict, with hearings held on three different dates. Finally, on September 10, 1970, Brower was found guilty of careless driving and lost his license for six months. Brower appealed his conviction, and it was reduced to three months.[110]

After Thomas Kavula was given a burial mass at the same church in which his parents were married, he was laid to rest at the Holy Cross Cemetery in North Arlington, New Jersey. His legacy endures through his daughter, Karen, and three grandchildren: Ashley, Meredith and Lauren.

STRUCK DOWN BY A DRUNK

ROBERT J. PRATO #2353

Troopers can empathize with the excitement that Robert Prato felt when opening his state police acceptance letter. Competition is fierce for the position of trooper. A member of the seventy-sixth class, Robert Prato is listed among those dying in the line of duty.[111]

Prato's family came from the state of Pennsylvania, where both of his parents were born and raised. Mother Lena (née Saini) and father James were of Italian descent. James lived in the town of Indiana, and Lena several miles down the road in Homer City. How the two met isn't certain; however, they settled down in Pennsylvania, like their parents before them. James and Lena had their first son, James, while living in Pennsylvania. As James grew up, he loved playing outdoors, and on a cold winter's day, he was out sleigh riding when tragedy struck. His sleigh drifted into the road, and he was struck and killed by a passing automobile. Words cannot describe the hurt and sorrow that the young couple felt. To ease their suffering, they moved to New Jersey.[112]

The Pratos took up residence in Bridgeton, which sits on the Cohansey River in south Jersey. A century before, Bridgeton had been a sawmill town, but since then, large Victorian homes had been built throughout the community. The town holds the distinction of being the largest historical district in the state.[113]

During this time, the couple had a second son, William. Then, in the winter of 1944, their third son, Robert John Prato, was born on December 6, 1944. One more child would follow, Elizabeth.[114]

Robert and Joann. *Courtesy of Joann Prato.*

The Pratos sent their children to the parochial grammar school Immaculate Conception. Robert's childhood wasn't much different from anyone else's. He played Little League, liked football and was mischievous at times. After completing his grammar school education, Robert was sent to the public high school in Bridgton. It was now September 1959, and the fourteen-year-old began caddying on weekends at a local golf course. This sparked an interest in the sport that remained with him throughout his life. In November, Prato met Joann Tansky in the hallway of school and started up a conversation with her. From that moment, an enduring relationship was formed. Joann was an attractive girl whose family were of Ukrainian and Polish descent. Throughout high school, Joann and Robert were inseparable.[115]

In high school, Prato played baseball and football and was an average student academically. Prato had an inviting personality and had a wide group of friends who all enjoyed social activities. Robert Prato and Joann Tansky graduated from Bridgeton High School in June 1963.[116]

The high school graduates enjoyed their newfound success and spent the summer of '63 together. By the fall, Prato had decided to enter the U.S. Air Force and enlisted. A year later, at the age of twenty, the two were wed in a ceremony on Saturday, October 10, 1964. At the time, Robert was stationed in Roswell, New Mexico, so Joann moved to New Mexico to be with him. In August 1965, Joann gave birth to their first child, a son named Robert. In the summer of 1966, Joann and Robert decided that it best for her and their son to move back to New Jersey and stay with Joann's parents while Prato finished his tour of service.[117]

In early 1967, Prato was a civilian and living back with his wife and son at his in-laws' home. He began working for Kimble Glass Plant in

A happy family. *Courtesy of Joann Prato.*

Vineland, New Jersey. This was the only job that he held before becoming a state trooper.[118]

Prato had taken the examination for becoming trooper at a time when the state police were in the news nearly every day. The year 1967 witnessed the outfit being called on to assist with the race riots that had taken hold in cities such as Newark, Jersey City and Plainfield. It wasn't uncommon to see Jersey troopers riding on fire trucks escorting firemen to calls or patrolling the city streets in their black-and-white troop cars. When the violence subsided, the organization walked away with accolades from municipal and state leaders. From these troubled times, formalized civil disturbance training for law enforcement throughout the state was initiated.[119]

About the time he received his acceptance letter into training, Joann gave birth to another son, Joseph. On Monday, October 28, the normal state police pomp and circumstance ushered Robert Prato into the state police.[120]

Prato reported to the Berlin Station, which is part of Troop A, and began his state police journey. With a secure and decent-paying job, he and Joann purchased a piece of property at 519 Manheim Avenue in Bridgeton and built a three-bedroom ranch complete with white paint and black shutters.[121]

Trooper Prato's second assignment was at Cape May Court House. Another transfer followed that sent him to the Mantua Station in Gloucester County.[122]

In February 1969, William Prato #2405 followed in his younger brother's footsteps and graduated from the seventy-seventh class. The siblings had always been close, but this increased their bond.[123]

According to Joann Prato, Robert's first year with the state police went by in a flash. Married now for five years, the couple still hadn't had a chance to travel or go on vacation. Their time, however, was always spent together, first with Robert and her and then the children. Robert had big plans for his children; he used to talk about getting them involved in sports and was excited about the prospect of coaching. Robert spent as much time with his kids as one possibly could working the demanding job of a trooper. Sadly, his dreams of a bright future were not to be.[124]

On the morning of Tuesday, December 2, 1969, Robert and Joann awoke to begin their day. It had been a long time since their meeting in school. He was about to turn twenty-five, and the couple had come a long way together. Joann remembered her last moments on this morning with her husband. "It was a nice, peaceful time together," she said. The children awoke early and spent time with Daddy. Prato was working the afternoon shift and had to be there at 2:00 p.m. As it neared one o'clock in the afternoon, Robert Prato kissed Joann and his children goodbye and headed off.[125]

Detailed to Interstate 295, records place Trooper Robert Prato in car A-220, which was a 1968 Ford. The night was clear with cold temperatures as Prato cruised in his troop car. Thus far, the afternoon and night had been quiet, and presumably Prato was "looping" his assigned area (a common

Left to right: Dad, Robert, William and Mom.
Courtesy of Joann Prato.

practice with highway assignments to ensure that motorists are not in need of assistance).[126]

Trooper Prato was driving in the far left lane, unaware that a vehicle was traveling the wrong way heading toward him in that same lane. By the time Prato spotted the car, it was too late. He braked abruptly, leaving more than one hundred feet of skid marks before the impact. Trooper J.J. Guzzardo #2107 was on patrol and heard a voice come over the radio: "Help me Bill, help me." Sadly, these were the last words uttered by Robert Prato (could he have been calling for his brother?). Guzzardo picked up his microphone and asked Prato for his location. There was no reply.[127]

On Saturday, December 6, 1969, a day that was to be his twenty-fifth birthday, Robert John Prato was laid to rest at Saint Mary's Cemetery in Bridgeton.[128]

A postscript to this story is that on April 7, 1995, Prato's youngest son, Joseph, became a trooper as a graduating member of the 115th class. A little over a year later, the Bridgeton State Police Station was dedicated to Trooper Robert Prato #2353, with the Prato family there to honor their loved one. Today, Detective Joseph Prato #5309 is a supervisor with the Evidence Management Unit.[129]

TRAIN CROSSING

RUSSELL J. MOESTA #2579

Trooper Russell Moesta's parents were from Philadelphia, Pennsylvania. His father, also named Russell, was of German heritage and was a veteran of the United States Marine Corps. Russell met an Englishwoman named Lillian Elmirah Cary, and the two fell in love and married on Saturday, February 26, 1938. The marriage produced three daughters, Lilyan, Audrey Ann and Cheryl, and one son, Russell, who was born on Sunday, January 7, 1945.[130]

In July 1948, the Moestas moved to a house on Tomlin Avenue in Atlantic City, New Jersey, when Russell became unemployed from a job he held in Philadelphia. Once in Atlantic City, Russell began working for the *Atlantic City Press* newspaper. Lillian remained a stay-at-home mother. The couple enjoyed living in Atlantic City and spent hours on the pristine beaches there. Atlantic City is located on Absecon Island and once was the summer vacation spot for the Leni-Lenape Indians. After dinner, the family would take walks on the beach. They loved watching the kids play while relaxing—a tradition that lasted for years.[131]

The Moestas purchased a white two-story row home at 206 Parkside Avenue that boasted three bedrooms, a living room, a dining room, a kitchen and a bath and sat two blocks from the beach.[132]

Their children were growing like weeds, and Russell became the most anxious of the three. "Buddy," as his parents coined him, was filled with energy and loved rough-and-tumble activities. Buddy attended the public

Junior lifeguard (center). *Courtesy of Cheryl Moesta.*

schools of Madison Avenue Grammar and Central Junior High School. At an early age, Buddy showed an interest in the junior lifeguard patrol program. It was natural for him to seek a position as he spent many hours on the sands of the Absecon Channel at the beach at Maine and Caspian.[133]

In school, Buddy played baseball, but lifeguarding was his passion. Russell Sr. had developed diabetes, and because of his illness, medical bills mounted, causing him and Lillian to lose their home. The couple stayed in the city and rented an apartment at 2406 Atlantic Avenue. The couple remained strong for their children, and their faith carried them through. Every Sunday, the Moestas could be seen attending mass at the Saint James Episcopal Church where Buddy served as an altar boy. Despite their setbacks, they never lost hope or a devotion to the Lord.[134]

Buddy finally met his goal and became a lifeguard. As a guard, Moesta took advantage of the perks that lifeguarding brought—namely girls. He stood six feet, one inch tall and weighed nearly two hundred pounds. With his dark-brown hair, brown eyes and a constant tan, it was all he could do to keep the women away. However, one girl in particular caught his eye: Marie Gail Camp. He would fall in love with and marry her. There was another woman who had an impact on Moesta as well. Her name was Jana Perskie. Buddy and Marie had broken up when Jana came on the scene. Jana says the two were more friends than anything else. According to her, "Buddy is one of the rare people who served his community, state and country." She remembered Moesta receiving many awards for his lifesaving deeds. She also remembered other things about him as well: "He was a handsome man." But the most appealing part for her was his personality. She said that Moesta was a quiet man whose "thoughts ran deep."[135]

Cheryl Moesta remembered her brother being meticulous and obsessed with cleanliness. "When my mother was making sandwiches, if anyone came by her, he would refuse to eat it, saying, 'They breathed on it'…he refused to put clothes in the hamper because he wanted his washed separately." Her brother also brushed his teeth constantly, especially after drinking soda. These traits evolved into strong character traits of discipline and manner.[136]

By 1963, his family had moved to another apartment on Atlantic Avenue. In June, Moesta graduated near the top of his class. Russell adored his father and pursued the same professional career that his dad had chosen years before.[137]

In September, Moesta joined the United State Marines. By this time, his father was in frail health, but knowing that his son was going to be a marine lifted his spirits.[138]

The Marine Corps dates back to 1775 with the Continental marines and the fight for American freedom. The first recruiting post was a place called Tun Tavern, located in Philadelphia. Moesta's first assignment was Camp LeJeune. In December, his father became gravely ill, and fortunately, Buddy came home on leave on December 23 and got to see his father. His father had hung on in the hopes of seeing his son. The very next day, on Christmas Eve, Russell Moesta Sr. passed away.[139]

Loving father. *Courtesy of Cheryl Moesta.*

In January 1964, Marie and Buddy were married, and a brief honeymoon followed. Moesta returned to base, and Marie stayed with her parents but eventually moved to the base with him. Moesta was transferred to the Brooklyn, New York Navy Yard, where he became a brig guard. He liked this position of authority, and it is believed to be the reason why he chose the state police upon leaving the military.[140]

In February 1965, a son was born, Christopher, and two years later, in 1967, Moesta left the service. The most rewarding achievement of being a marine was the joy of seeing his father's face when he graduated the Marine Corps. Marines have a saying, "Once a marine, always a marine." In the near future, the young man would seek out an organization with similar core beliefs.[141]

Buddy and Gail, as he called her, were living with her parents while he worked for the J.P. Mooney's Florist as a deliveryman. During the summer, Buddy began lifeguarding. In April 1969, Gail became pregnant, and a few months later, Russell took the entrance examination for the state police.[142]

In December, Buddy's close friend since boyhood, Tommy Sciuto, passed away. The two men had remained close throughout the years. Many times, Buddy and his sister, Cheryl, would go over to Tommy's house and eat his mother's meatballs. In fact, one of the first things Buddy did with Gail after they married was to bring her to Mrs. Sciuto's house to try her meatballs. The loss of Tommy was contrasted in emotions by the birth of his son, Dennis, the very next day. The couple spent the holiday season with their boys, hopeful that the state police job would come through. Two months later, their hopes were fulfilled, and on February 8, 1970, Russell Moesta entered training as a member of the eighty-first class. Fourteen weeks later, Russell Moesta was named outstanding recruit and received a special award of excellence in academic achievement, marksmanship, physical fitness and character traits. It was a wonderful start to what was to be a promising career. Trooper Russell Moesta #2579 was detailed to Port Norris in Troop A.[143]

A trademark of Jersey troopers is their ability to conduct investigations. Many agencies don't allow uniformed officers to conduct full investigations. In the New Jersey State Police, it is expected. History records Trooper Russell Moesta exercising this authority on November 19, 1970.[144]

The twenty-five-year-old trooper was sinking his teeth into a robbery investigation that involved two white males. Of the two suspects, Moesta identified Joseph Ritchie, a local troublemaker, as a prime suspect. Ritchie was in the county jail on an unrelated charge, and Moesta arranged a suspect lineup on this particular day.[145]

Trooper Moesta was operating troop car A-840 on Ramah Road in Fairfield Township. State records indicate that Moesta's speed was above the posted limit as he drove. A presumption can be made that Moesta was aware that he was approaching a railroad crossing, as signs were visible on Ramah Road of such an intersection. However, several large homes and one large tree prevented a clear view of the tracks. As he neared the intersection, so did a locomotive pulling seventy-eight boxcars and a sand hopper. Train operator Carmen Gettis spotted Moesta and "sounded several short blasts" on his horn to warn him. Nearly 156 feet of "heavy skid marks" were left by the troop car as it met the locomotive. The train dragged the police cruiser 79 feet before setting it free and leaving Trooper Moesta dead behind his steering wheel.[146]

Russell John Moesta was buried three days before Thanksgiving on Monday, November 23. His final resting place is next to his father at the Egg Harbor City Cemetery on Moss Mill Road.[147]

CALL ME RENNIE

MARIENUS J. SEGEREN #2414

In 2010, illegal immigration was in the news nearly every day. Since September 11, officials in border states with Mexico have been questioning the U.S. policies on securing our borders. An even older debate has stirred anew with what to do with those already here illegally, as well as with their children born in the United States. The story of Marienus Segeren has its roots in this issue.[148]

Trooper Marienus Segeren's father, also named Marienus, was born circa 1910 in London, England, and raised in Holland. The Segeren family roots are derived from England, Ireland, Germany and Holland. Marienus's father grew up in Holland, and at the age of twelve, his father obtained an apprenticeship for him as an electrician. The electrician's apprentice didn't care much for the vocation, nor for that matter his father. So, at the age of fifteen, Marienus's father took a job as a cabin boy on a ship setting out to Austria. Big plans were visualized by the teenager, but when he became seasick, the stopover in America set his family's destiny.[149]

The ship anchored in New York, where the immigrant population enabled the teenager to assimilate. The first few years were tough, with little known of his trials and tribulations. Presumably he lived on the streets. One of the first things he did was change his name to Charles. (He hated the name "Marienus.") Whether that disdain came from the name itself or from his hatred for his father is unknown. Charles Segeren obtained a job working in a factory and then at the Campbell Soup Company as an engineer.[150]

Rennie, Charlie, Elaine and their mother. *Courtesy of Lynne (Segeren) Freedman.*

Somewhere in time, Charles met Constance Ida Earhardt, a woman of German descent whose parents changed the spelling of their name so as to not be stigmatized because of Hitler's power-hungry ambitions. The family simply dropped the "t" from the spelling, making the pronunciation sound less German. The couple married and had three children: Elaine, Charles and Marienus. Interestingly, even though Charles hated the Marienus name, his last born child bore that name. Marienus James Segeren, born on April 30, 1941, is the subject of this narrative.[151]

Charles and Constance lived in Little Ferry, New Jersey, as well as in Pennsylvania, before settling in Camden, New Jersey. From an early age, their son Marienus wanted to be a Jersey trooper. It was a passion that remained with him through adolescence, into high school and then into adulthood. The family was living at 3046 Fenwick Road in a part of Camden known as the Fairview Section. Here Marienus received the bulk of his education.[152]

Lynne Marlow was a sixth grader sitting in class when the principal walked in with a boy she didn't recognize. "We have a new student," said the principal. "His name is Marienus Segeren." Quickly, without hesitation, the boy said, "No, call me Rennie." The principal responded, "Oh, ok…his name is Rennie." This was the moment Lynne laid eyes on the person she would someday marry.[153]

Lynne Marlow was born on April 3, 1941, to Cyril and Alberta Sara (née Redmond), who were of English, Irish and German descent. Her family lived in Camden and were of a modest income. Her father, like Rennie's, came to America at the age of fifteen. Later on in life, he worked for a newspaper and authored a book.[154]

As a child, Rennie enjoyed riding bicycles, ice skating and playing basketball. "I had a crush on him," said Lynne. They used to play together, and the two became close friends. At fifteen, Lynne's family moved a few towns away, and she saw Rennie from time to time at dances. Rennie "loved to dance and was good at it…he could do the twist like no one before." However, it wasn't until a mutual friend set them up on a formal date that things began to evolve into a courtship.[155]

For years Lynne had a crush on him; whether he knew this or not is uncertain. That first true date took place at a local eatery in Camden, and when it ended, Rennie walked her to the door and kissed her on the cheek. "Wow," Lynne thought, "a real gentleman." Rennie was her soul mate.[156]

The year was 1960, and at nineteen years of age, with blue eyes and brown hair, Rennie stood nearly five feet, ten inches, and weighed only 157 pounds. Most often he sported the scruffy look because he hated to shave. After a year of dating, the couple eloped.[157]

With only a few hundred dollars in hand, the couple headed south and spent the night in a Florence, South Carolina hotel, where that night they rolled their change to bring to the bank for paper money. The next day, they "went to a judge and told him we wanted to get married by a clergy," said Lynne. The town was old-fashioned, with a welcoming feel to it. The judge put together a ceremony and used his little daughter as the ring bearer. "He gave me away," said Lynne, laughing. The ceremony took place at about one o'clock in the afternoon on August 25, 1961. "It was a beautiful day," said Lynne. "I was so excited and so nervous."[158]

The young married man begun studying electrical engineering at the Spring Garden Institute in Philadelphia, which really contrasted with his ambition to be a trooper. "That's all he ever wanted to do," said Lynne. "From when he was a kid, he wanted to be a state trooper. He used to talk about it." His study in electrical engineering was probably rooted in his father's early electrician's apprenticeship. During this time, Rennie was working part time bartending.[159]

At this point, the couple was living in a duplex apartment on Prospect Road in Haddonfield, New Jersey. The marriage of the two bore three children: Jodi Lynne was born in April 1962, Rennie Marlow in June 1963 and Terri in October 1965. In late 1965, the apartment became too small, and they purchased a twin home on the corner of Fourth and Walnut in Haddonfield. This house was in need of remodeling, with Rennie taking to that task. When he cut short a large piece of linoleum, turning a small project into a major one, Lynne realized that her husband wasn't much of a craftsman. "Neighbors in the next house used to make fun of him…he was not handy," she laughed. But "he tried everything." Soon, their fourth and final child, Jill, was born in January 1967. With this large family, Rennie began working for the Langston Company as a material handler. while keeping his part-time bartender position. Shortly after Jill's birth, Lynne's father became gravely ill, so they sold their home to move in with her parents.[160]

Rennie's dream of becoming a trooper had been put on hold for years. "We had to save enough money so we could live well enough with the children while he went to the academy," said Lynne. The couple purchased the second home, a bungalow with a "lovely front porch," at 321 Walnut Avenue in Oaklyn, New Jersey.[161]

Rennie always kept himself in shape by weight training, doing pushups and situps and running, which was a passion of his, putting in ten miles a day.[162] By the summer of 1968, Rennie and his wife had enough money

Easter 1970: Dad with (left to right) Jodi, Terri, Rennie and Jill. *Courtesy of Lynne (Segeren) Freedman.*

for him to try for the job he really wanted. He took the state police examination and passed. In October, his acceptance letter to begin training at Sea Girt arrived.[163]

In November, Rennie began training, which put a terrific strain on him and Lynne both. While he was enduring the physicality of training, Lynne was caring for their children. This would be an introduction to her of the difficulties of being the wife of a Jersey trooper: lonely nights, empty holidays and learning to be independent.[164]

On Friday, February 7, 1969, Rennie graduated as a member of the seventy-seventh class with badge #2414. Graduating along with him was Trooper Robert Merenda #2393. Bob Merenda and Rennie became best friends, with both of their state police careers concluding in tragedy.[165]

Rennie Segeren and Bob Merenda reported to Troop A headquarters the following Monday, with Rennie being assigned to the Tuckerton Station.[166]

Trooper Segeren had tours at the Mays Landing and Malaga Stations before being transferred to the Atlantic City Expressway. In his personal life, Rennie loved to work outside and became friendly with the children in the neighborhood. "When he came home," said Lynne, "he was a husband and a dad…I was a very hesitant mother, but he wasn't…He enjoyed his kids." As their tenth anniversary neared, the difficulties of being a trooper's wife were increasing. "It was terrible on our marriage," said Lynne. "I was disgusted with the job…I can see where it can ruin relationships." The job required long hours, and Lynne said that it was a "tough life for [her]." It was also difficult on him, "but it was nice when he was home," she said.. "I know he missed us terrible" when he was at work; "it tore him apart."[167]

When off duty, Rennie focused on his family and enjoyed hobbies such as watching football. Rennie was a conversationalist and enjoyed spending time with Lynne and their friends. In April 1971, the couple celebrated their thirtieth birthdays; Lynne happened to be two weeks older, and Rennie never let her forget it.[168]

In spite of the difficulties, Rennie Segeren truly loved being a trooper. He did his job well and worked hard to better himself. In the early morning hours of Sunday, July 25, 1971, all of his hard work and success would come to an end.[169]

Trooper Segeren had slept well before his shift. Prior to work, he stopped in the town of Ventnor to listen to a musical group that was playing on the beach. The Atlantic City Expressway is a difficult and dangerous road to patrol. Oftentimes, weekend nights are filled with disputes and drunk drivers. Sunday nights always seemed to be busier than any others.[170]

Rennie and Lynne. *Courtesy of Lynne (Segeren) Freedman.*

Trooper Segeren arrived at 10:30 p.m. and, twenty minutes later, was out in his 1971 Dodge troop car, ACE-30, patrolling the roadway. The first contact for him came at 10:59 p.m., which was a motorist aid. As expected, it was a busy night, with a number of broken-down vehicles, tickets issued and a drunk driver arrest made by Segeren. By the end of the shift, fatigue had hit the trooper hard.[171]

While driving, he fell asleep at milepost 21.6 in the westbound lanes of the expressway and veered off the roadway. His troop car hit the milepost marker. Records indicate that this woke Segeren from his sleep, and he turned sharply to get back onto the road. This caused him to spin out of control, crossing the entire westbound lanes and hitting the guardrail and then two concrete support pillars for the Weymouth-Elwood Road overpass.[172]

Lynne Segeren was normally a sound sleeper, but for some reason, on this particular night she couldn't sleep. "I had a horrible feeling," she said. During the night, she checked her phone several times to see if it was working. At 6:05 a.m., Lynne thought she heard the phone ring and picked it up. She laid back down and dozed off. "I can't tell you the feeling I had," she said. Then a knock came at the door. It was their good friend Trooper Cliff Disney #2374, as well as another trooper. In the early morning hours, when most people are asleep, a wife of a Jersey trooper was being told of her husband's demise. The time of his death was determined to be 6:05 a.m.[173]

"After I lost Rennie." Lynne said, "I couldn't understand how the world continued…they announced his death on the TV news, and then continued on with other news." How could they do that? "But after you get through that, you will do ok…You have to go on because you have the kids, so you have to go on, so you do." Rennie's death made Lynne question her faith: "I didn't believe in God anymore." Even more troubling for the grieving widow were her feelings toward the state police. "I blamed the troopers for his death," recalled Lynne. Looking back fondly on her husband, Lynne said that Rennie "was such a good person who never met anyone he didn't like." If he did, he never mentioned it. "I know it sounds impossible, but he never said anything bad about anyone."[174]

Rennie Segeren left this earth at the early age of thirty; his legacy lives on through thirteen grandchildren.

IT CAN'T HAPPEN TO HIM!

ROBERT J. MERENDA #2393

B ob Merenda was a man's man—strong, athletic and charismatic. He was a high school All-Catholic League halfback. In college, he was an athlete who caught the eye of the Denver Broncos. And as a trooper, he was a role model to a young kid named Jim Principe. During his lifetime, Merenda touched many lives and was a man of tremendous ambitions, illustrated by his numerous list of jobs: lifeguard, bartender, floor man, busboy, lube man, rental agent, cement worker, construction foreman and salesman. Simply stated, Bob Merenda was an individual with great aspirations and a hard work ethic used to achieve those aspirations. Trooper Robert Merenda #2393 was a husband, father, friend and role model.[175]

Robert Joseph Merenda was born on Saturday, September 9, 1939, in the sandy beach community of Seaside Park, New Jersey. Seaside Park is situated in Ocean County and is part of the Barnegat Peninsula, which separates Barnegat Bay from the Atlantic Ocean. Merenda was born at a time when Seaside Park had fewer than six hundred people; now the town has nearly three thousand residents. The Merendas eventually settled in Audubon, New Jersey, which sits next to the Delaware River looking across at the city of Philadelphia. Robert and Mae Merenda were devout Catholics. When Merenda was school age, his parents sent him to the public grammar school. Upon graduating, he was then given a parochial education attending West Catholic High School in Philadelphia. While there, Merenda excelled at football. He was a halfback and rose to be the team's captain.[176]

Robert Merenda #2393. *Courtesy of the New Jersey State Police.*

By the summer of his graduating year, Merenda was working as a lifeguard with Wildwood's Beach Patrol. Tall, with "blue piercing eyes," sandy brown hair and a personality that would consume you, Merenda was a popular guard. Wildwood is known for its wide, sandy beaches, and was a nice summer job for the man. The summer of 1958 was filled with nice weather and hit songs such as Bobby Darin's song "Splish Splash." In November, Merenda began working as a lube man for the Merlin Motor Company in Camden. During this period, Merenda applied to Villanova University in Pennsylvania.[177]

It was only a matter of time before he had a place on its football team. Merenda's college football career is worth mentioning, not only for Merenda's play but also for the team's successful season. Two highlights of this season were when the team played the Liberty Bowl in Philadelphia against Oregon State University and when it played in the Sun Bowl against Wichita State. During the Liberty Bowl game, the weather was so brutally cold (seventeen degrees at kick off) that the field was rock hard, which forced players to wear sneakers instead of their traditional cleats. The game was telecast on national TV and was seen by an estimated 27 million people. Interestingly, a ninety-nine-yard touchdown run during the game by Terry Baker, a future Heisman winner, still holds the record. For Merenda, his performance caught the eye of a professional scout, which led to a professional albeit short-lived football career.[178]

In July 1963, the twenty-three-year-old was drafted by the Denver Broncos; the organization paid him $50 per game and promised him a salary of $8,600 if he made it onto the team. Bob Merenda played through September but was ultimately let go. Next came a minor-league position on the Daytona Beach Football Club in Florida. He played throughout the 1963 season.[179]

After Daytona, Merenda's football career appeared to be over, so he returned home. He began working for Anthony Garguile and Sons out of Sharon Hill, Pennsylvania. Merenda worked for this construction company up until Thanksgiving 1964, when he quit. The football itch sprouted up once again. Bob Merenda tried out for the Continental Football League (CFL), which was formed in early 1965. The CFL was a minor league that put together ten teams, with one of them being the Newark Bears. Merenda joined the Bears in July, and they paid him $150 per game. Unfortunately, an elbow injury took him off the team. He landed on his feet, aided and abetted by the management staff of the Bears, and got a job at the McGregor Dowiger Sports Company in Dover, New Jersey. This position brought a weekly paycheck of $110.[180]

By the summer of 1966, Merenda had begun dating Nancy Doris, a young woman who had caught his eye. He had also started working again for Anthony Garguile; he was promoted to assistant foreman. History would record Bob Merenda strapping on a football helmet one last time.[181]

At the age of twenty-six, a tryout for the Philadelphia Bulldogs, a minor-league team, put Merenda on the team roster. In addition to playing football, Bob worked off hours at Spano Real Estate in Springfield, Pennsylvania. Essentially, he was working two jobs and bringing in a considerable amount of cash, much more than any trooper patrolling the streets of New Jersey was making at the time. Merenda played the entire season with the Bulldogs but was let go after the season ended. Merenda's football career had come to a close. But another opportunity was on the horizon.[182]

Having joined the seventy-seventh state police class, Bob Merenda graduated on Monday, February 3, 1969, with badge #2393. The year 1969 was an important one for the outfit. In May, under the leadership of Colonial D.B. Kelly, the newly formed Helicopter Bureau began training. For the young trooper, this was the least of his concerns, as he had a job to learn. His first station was in Troop A.[183]

Hammonton Station is named after the town of Hammonton, which was founded in 1857 by Charles K. Landis. Landis was a brilliant man who was educated as an attorney and became a developer. His first endeavor was the development of Hammonton. Other towns developed by Landis included Vineland, Millville and Sea Isle City. Bizarrely, when a newspaper wrote disparaging words about Landis's wife's apparent mental condition, Landis walked into the editor's office with a gun and shot the man in the head. Landis pleaded not guilty by reason of insanity, marking an early case in judicial history during which this defense was used. The trial gained national attention in 1876 with Landis being found not guilty.[184]

After Hammonton, Merenda had tours at the Red Lion and Woodstown Stations before being sent to the New Jersey Turnpike, known as Troop D.[185]

James Principe, a retired New Jersey state trooper, has fond memories of Bob Merenda and credits him with being his role model and inspiration for becoming a Jersey trooper. Nancy was Principe's cousin, and from the moment Principe met Merenda, a lasting impression was formed. "He was like the Hulk," said Principe. "He had twenty-two-inch arms and was just an impressive type of individual." Principe was enthralled with Merenda's state police stories.[186]

Ronald Perozzi was Bob Merenda's line partner, and he said that Merenda "was a physical specimen, a man's man." The two met working out of Moorestown while patrolling the southern portion of the turnpike. Ron and Bob became close friends. Perozzi had fond memories. "Bob would have you in stitches...one of the greatest guys I have ever met in my life," said Perozzi. In fact, Merenda had many friends, and although Ron didn't know if Bob considered him his best friend, Perozzi said that "he was mine." On duty, the two would have breakfast and lunch together. After work, the two hung out together. At night, the two rode together. (Two-man patrols are required at night.) "We just palled around as much as we could," Perozzi said.[187]

By now, Bob and Nancy had married and purchased a home at 143 Yale Road in Audubon, New Jersey. The couple's first son, Robert, was born in 1970. In March 1971, the couple's last child, Scott, was born. Bob Merenda had come a long way from working odd jobs, but now he was happy and had a good job and a wonderful family. By year's end, the couple wanted to celebrate Thanksgiving with friends, so Perozzi received an invitation.

"I was divorced at the time," said Perozzi. "I was alone...[and] had already committed." This, sadly, was the last opportunity he would have had to spend a holiday with his friend. Thanksgiving came on the twenty-fifth of 1971 and was a wonderful day spent eating, enjoying family and watching TV. Bob, Nancy and the children went to bed with full stomachs and joy in their hearts.[188]

The story that follows has been told before with slight changes in the levels of contempt, negligence or inattentiveness; regardless, the outcome is the same. Troopers have paid the ultimate sacrifice due to the carelessness of others, and Bob Merenda's elegy concluded the same way.[189]

In the early morning hours of Monday, November 29, 1971, Trooper Merenda was citing a motorist for speeding at milepost 13.2 on the southbound side of the turnpike. Merenda had stopped the vehicle for speeding, and while he was walking to the car to give the motorist a ticket, he was struck and killed by a twenty-two-year-old female driver who had fallen asleep at the wheel. Robert Merenda was pronounced dead upon arrival at Underwood Hospital in Woodbury.[190]

A short time later, a teenage boy was sitting in his high school classroom when his father arrived. "I remember the day my father came to school... it was right after the Thanksgiving football game my senior year...they called me out of the classroom to the principle's office." When told of Bob Merenda having been struck by a car, the teenage Principe's first thought was, "Gee, what happened to the car?...He was so bigger than life to me." With a crackle in his throat, Ron Perozzi said, "I couldn't imagine that he could be killed...he was just an awesome specimen of a man."[191]

SHOOTOUT WITH THE BLACK LIBERATION ARMY

WERNER FOERSTER #2608

It was a quiet start to what would be a historic night for the New Jersey State Police. Troopers Robert Palentchar #1946, James Harper #2108 and Werner Foerster #2608 were given their assignments. Foerster had the northern area, Palentchar the southern portion and Harper the middle. These men worked out of one of the three stations responsible for providing services to the New Jersey Turnpike. Newark and Moorestown are the other two. New Brunswick was the center station for this busy and dangerous superhighway and sat south of Interchange 9. (Today the facility serves as an administrative office for the New Jersey Turnpike.) After assignments, the three men headed out the door. Werner Foerster loaded his blue-and-white troop car 820 and proceeded north. Not long afterward, Foerster was detailed to pick up an item from an interchange and relay it back to the station. Trooper Ronald Foster #2240, who was working the station record and serving as dispatcher, remembered this night all to well. He spoke with Werner when he came back to the station and remembered Foerster being anxious to resume patrol before a call came in.[192]

While doing administrative work, Ron Foster was startled when the radio sounded. Trooper Harper was calling in a motor vehicle stop—"an early 1960 [white] Pontiac, 2-door; occupied by two black males and one black female." The stop took place at milepost 83 south at the foot of the station's driveway, only a few hundred feet from where Foster sat. "I radioed to Bob Palentchar to back up Harper," recalled Foster, "but he did not answer and

Werner picked up the call." Foerster hadn't traveled far and hit the next U-turn to back up Harper. Upon arriving at Harper's location, Foerster pulled behind Harper's Oldsmobile, troop car 894, and got out without telling the station of his arrival.[193]

Foerster observed Harper talking with the front passenger and the driver standing in front of Harper's troop car. Harper had noted "a discrepancy in the registration" and had asked the driver (later identified as Clark E. Squire) to step out of the car and move to the front of his troop car. He spoke briefly with him before leaving to speak with the other occupants of the vehicle. This is when Foerster pulled up. The front-seat passenger told Harper that her name was Maureen Jones; however, her name was actually Joanne Chesimard, the "revolutionary mother hen of the Black Liberation Army" (BLA). As Harper spoke with Chesimard, Werner Foerster performed a protective pat-down on Squire and found a loaded gun clip on him. Apparently, as Foerster was performing the pat-down, Harper was noticing that Chesimard kept her hand in her purse. Then, imprudently, Werner supposedly yelled to Harper that he had found an ammo clip. With that utterance, Chesimard pulled out a loaded semiautomatic handgun and shot Harper in the shoulder.

Under continuous fire from her weapon, and after being struck, Harper managed to draw his weapon and return fire while tactically retreating toward his troop car. A vicious firefight got underway, with Werner Foerster and Clark Squire fighting in the middle. Chesimard exited her vehicle with gun blazing, as did the back-seat passenger, James F. Coston. He, too, had a weapon. As the two exited their car, Harper shot at both, dropping Chesimard to the ground and striking Coston with what was to be a mortal wound. Despite being shot and on the ground, the BLA leader continued to shoot and turned her attention to Foerster, hitting him in the chest and the right arm. Harper had exhausted his rounds from his inferior six-shot revolver and was forced to retreat toward the state police station.[194]

Alone, lying on the ground, Foerster was executed with two bullets to the back of his head. Supposedly, Chesimard is the one who pulled the trigger.[195]

As the BLA members drove south, Harper—apparently in shock— walked calmly into the station (leaving Ron Foster to believe that Harper had cleared from his motor vehicle stop). Foster said, "Jimmy comes into the station and says, 'Ron, you better put more troops out there; those people have guns.'" Foster laughed, thinking that Harper was taking a crack at the lack of a police presence on the road that night. "Jimmy," Ron replied, "all those people out there now carry guns." However, Harper's response was, "Yeah, but they just shot me." Turning, James Harper showed his bleeding bullet wound to his colleague. At no time did Harper mention Werner Foerster being out with him. Presumably, Harper assumed that Foerster had called out with him. However, he did not, leaving everyone to assume that Foerster was out on patrol. (Regardless, a quick response would have been futile in light of the coldblooded execution.)[196]

Working on information that Harper had initially called in, Trooper Palentchar found the car, with Clark Squire standing near the vehicle at milepost 78 south. Seeing the trooper, Squire fled into the woods, with Palentchar firing a round at him. Then, out of the corner of his eye, Palentchar saw Chesimard walking with her hands in the air. A closer inspection of the woman revealed that she was seriously wounded. Discovered a short distance from her was the body of James Coston.[197]

Werner Foerster #2608. *Courtesy of the New Jersey State Police.*

In the aftermath, much was written of the shooting and of Joanne Chesimard. Justice was swift for James Coston. For Clark Squire, his punishment was life behind bars. Joanne Chesimard received the same sentence, and she was sent away. However, state officials failed to see the threat that Chesimard and her BLA associates posed, and she was placed in the Clinton Correctional Facility for Women. In November 1979, a group of radical domestic terrorists took two prison guards hostage and broke Chesimard out of the minimum-security facility. Subsequently, Chesimard fled to Cuba and was granted political asylum under the government of Fidel Castro.[198]

In all the words written about the shooting, little has been recorded about Werner Foerster, a Jersey trooper, husband and father. Unfortunately, this is to remain. The trauma of losing Werner is still fresh in the memory of his wife, Rosa. As such, she did not want to speak about or provide any information about her husband. A look into the state police files isn't helpful, either. Let's explore what *is* known of the man.[199]

Werner Foerster became a Jersey trooper late in life—a life begun far from the Jersey Shores, in the city of Leipzig in the German state of Saxony. The future trooper was born on August 19, 1938. At the time, Germany was under Hitler's full control and was the center of the world's attention. Germany's military might was being carefully watched by the United States. The effects this had on the Foerster family aren't known, nor is it known how long they remained in Germany before immigrating to America.[200]

Foerster was educated through high school. As a man, he stood five feet, eight and a half inches tall and weighed less than 160 pounds. He had blond hair, blue eyes, a fair complexion and spoke with a German accent. In December 1963, Werner entered the United States Army and served in Vietnam.[201]

On November 18, 1964, at the age of twenty-six, Foerster married a German woman named Rosa Charlotte Heider. In December 1965, Foerster concluded his military service. He and Rosa moved to Marboro Road in Old Bridge, New Jersey. Foerster was a welder by trade and worked for Ross Engineering in New Brunswick. While going through the selection process to be accepted into the academy, Rosa became pregnant. On September 22, 1969, the couple's only child, Eric, was born.[202]

On April 20, 1970, sixty-two people entered training for the eighty-second state police class; fourteen weeks later, on July 24, forty men stood as troopers. The German-speaking former welder bore badge #2608.[203]

Monday, July 27, was Werner Foerster's first day working as a trooper. His first assignment was at the Toms River Station. During the next two years, Foerster worked out of the Colts Neck, Fort Dix and Keyport Stations.[204]

A week before Thanksgiving 1972, Foerster began patrolling the New Jersey Turnpike. Only a few months stood between him and his encounter with the Black Liberation Army.[205]

DETECTIVE

THOMAS A. DAWSON #2141

Thomas Atkins Dawson was born to Herbert and Francis. Herbert was of Scottish and Welsh descent, and Francis had Irish roots. Francis had been previously married and had a son, Michael Mecanko, in 1931. Thomas and Francis Dawson had one child together, Thomas. The Dawsons' love for each other faded with the passing of years, and they, too, eventually divorced. Herbert remarried, having five additional children, and Francis married a man named Stanley Kornicowski, who became like a second father to Thomas.[206]

Stanley and Francis Kornicowski lived in Hamilton Square, which is named after Alexander Hamilton; this tract of land is rich in history, dating back to 1692, when it was once called Nottingham (named after the famed British village).[207]

Tom Dawson, born on January 24, 1942, grew up in this rural community and was an average boy who liked games and sports, as most kids his age do. Dawson was an average student and stayed out of trouble during his school years. Dawson attended the Joseph Steinert Memorial School and while there met and began dating Diane Luzier. This relationship bore a son, Thomas E., born in August 1959, just two months before Diane's seventeenth birthday. When the couple married isn't known. The brown-haired, brown-eyed young father stood six foot one and had a muscular frame, weighing a lean 180 pounds. Next to Dawson's high school graduation photo in his 1959 yearbook, it read, "I love my Motorcycle."

Thomas Dawson #2141. *Courtesy of Ingrid Dawson.*

After high school, Dawson became gainfully employed as a mechanical assembler for IBM at its Dayton, New Jersey plant; this was primarily the only job the young man had before becoming a Jersey trooper.[208]

Hobbies and interests of the young man ranged from volunteering at the Nottingham Fire Company in Hamilton Square to being a member of the German American Society Club.[209]

Needless to say, Dawson applied to the state police and became a graduating member of the seventy-first class with badge #2141. Dawson began patrolling as a trooper out of Troop C on August 29, 1966, out of the Howell Station. By this time in his life, Dawson's marriage to Diane had failed, and the two were separated, pending a divorce. This was a troubling time for the young trooper. Then, on January 29, 1967, Dawson accepted an invitation with a few trooper colleagues to go out for a few drinks after work. While sitting at the bar of a local tavern, an attractive blonde walked up and asked the bartender for a drink. Dawson stood up and offered to buy her a drink, as well as gave his seat to her. That woman's name was Ingrid Stomberg, a hairdresser in town. The two found it easy to talk to each other and had an enjoyable time together. At the end of the night, Dawson asked for her phone number. When the man called her, he said that he was working and just wanted to stop by to say hi. Ingrid remembered this meeting well: "He didn't tell me what he did for a living…he pulled up in a troop car and was in uniform." Although secure in his looks, Dawson presumably thought that the uniform would seal the deal. Thereafter the two became an item.[210]

In March 1967, Dawson was transferred to the New Brunswick Station in Troop D; however, on September 11, he was moved to the Edgewater Park Barracks.[211]

By his twenty-sixth birthday, Dawson's relationship with Ingrid was at its peak, and they were waiting for his divorce to become final so they could marry. Then Ingrid became pregnant and gave birth to their only child—a son, Sean—in June 1968. A week before Christmas of this year, Dawson was detached to conduct background checks on applicants wishing to become troopers. This made for a nice holiday season, with ample time off for him to spend with his loved ones. Then, in February 1969, Dawson received a transfer to the Investigation Section of the Narcotics Bureau—a job for which he had applied. Positions such as this are much sought after. Dawson's selection to this impressive unit was not happenstance. His performance bore out his work ethic. Dawson's uniform patrol concluded with him receiving a commendation that read, in part: "Tpr. T.A. Dawson's continuous outstanding service in line of duty, his keen observation, and alertness while on patrol [and] good police investigation and efforts resulted in solving numerous crimes."[212]

Detective work is much different than in-uniform patrol. For some, this transition is often difficult. As it turned out, Dawson's transition was seamless. Working as a "Narco" detective is a dirty job within the state police—one of the least glamorous of all "specialized" units. Detectives work undercover in shady areas of the state, from rural, drug-infested communities to the inner city ghettos. Narco detectives often conduct complex investigations, but the bread and butter of the operation is on the street. Working these street operations often leads to bigger investigations. Although this position had demanding hours, it was still a better schedule for a man with a family than that of working in uniform.[213]

Dawson and Ingrid married on October 18, 1969, in a service taking place at the Saint Andrew by the Sea Lutheran Church in Atlantic City. A reception followed, with a long honeymoon in Puerto Rico and Saint Thomas Island. The newlyweds moved to 5 Dey Street in Englishtown, a two-family home owned by Ingrid's mother. The Dawsons lived upstairs, with her mother staying downstairs. Soon

Undercover. *Courtesy of Ingrid Dawson.*

Ingrid, Sean and Thomas. *Courtesy of Ingrid Dawson.*

thereafter, the Dawsons built a house next door at 7 Dey Street, where they had Ingrid's hairstyling business downstairs and lived in the upstairs apartment. However, this stay was short-lived, and they moved in the early 1970s to an apartment at Princeton Hightstown Apartments in Hightstown.[214]

Tommy Dawson enjoyed his family and remained close to his son, Thomas, who did not live with him but would visit. Dawson kept himself in shape and enjoyed working out. A passion of his was martial arts training. He practiced the art created by the legendary Bruce Lee. Jeet Kune Do was a system that blended different arts into one. Dawson became an expert in the art, achieving the rank of black belt. His wife, Ingrid, spoke of his skills in an incident that took place between Dawson and another trooper. The man was obnoxious and kept pushing Dawson, until blows were exchanged. It didn't take long before Dawson laid the man out. As a martial artist during the 1970s, Dawson was an admirer of Bruce Lee. However, as a participant of Lee's personal art, Dawson felt a closeness to the man that only a Jeet Kune Do practitioner could understand. So when the news on July 20, 1973, announced the death of Bruce Lee, it hit Dawson like a karate blow. Presumably, he thought that one day he himself would have the opportunity to meet the legendary martial artist; Ingrid said that her husband was beside

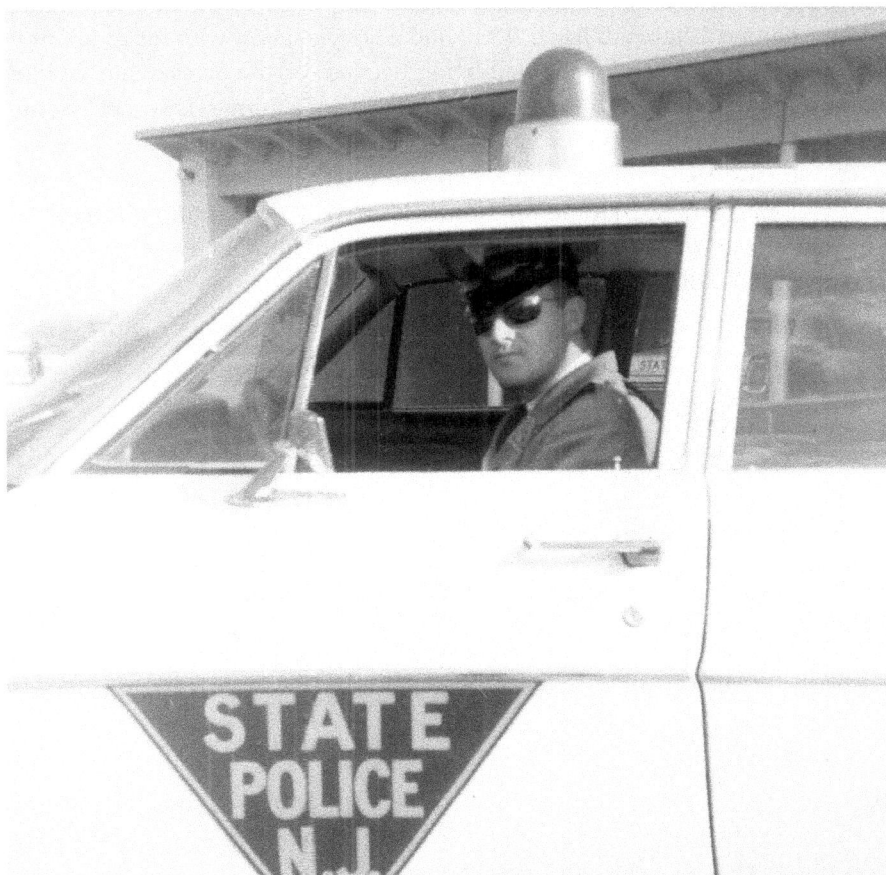

Heading out on patrol. *Courtesy of Ingrid Dawson.*

himself over it. Being a trooper in the state police leaves little time to wallow in the mire, so by late summer, Detective Dawson was engrossed in an active narcotics investigation that was consuming his time.[215]

On Monday, August 13, Tom had been working all day and was heading home a little after 11:00 p.m. Traveling on U.S. 130 in Washington Township in unmarked troop car U-2028, Dawson ran off the road and struck a tree. Some speculate that he was working on a case and was forced off the road by those involved. The investigation revealed a considerable amount of skid marks on the roadway prior to where Dawson's troop car left the road. Interestingly, Dawson's gun was never recovered from the crash scene despite an intense search. Moreover, "several rounds of [unspent] .380 ammunition was found at the scene." Years before Dawson's tenure in the outfit, a young trooper named Charley Ullrich #232 had a conversation with his mom. She had stressed a concern for his well-being because of the arrests that he had made. Could this have been what happened to Thomas Dawson? Some believe it is a possibility.[216]

The funeral for Thomas Atkins Dawson took place on August 17 at the Saul Colonial Funeral Home on Nottingham Way in Hamilton Township. The sadness of the day was highlighted by little Thomas Dawson yelling, "That's my Daddy! That's my Daddy!"[217]

TROOPER OF THE YEAR

PHILIP J. LAMONACO #2663

If they could get him, they could get anybody.
—former trooper John Delesio[218]

Philip Lamonaco was a heroic figure within the state police; troopers from north Jersey to the sandy beaches of Cape May knew his name. Citizens where he patrolled loved him, and local riffraff feared him. Phil Lamonaco loved wearing the uniform of a Jersey trooper and left a prestigious detective position to return to "the road" despite severe criticism.[219]

Born in Jersey City, New Jersey, Lamonaco was raised in the suburb of Roselle Park, which is part of Union County. Roselle Park is an intimate neighborhood where everyone knows one another. The community itself dates back to the 1700s, when the Galloping Hill Road running through town was used by Continental scouts in the Revolutionary War. Philip's parents, Joseph and Grace (née Ciccone), were of Italian descent. Joseph was a first-generation American, whereas Grace was second generation. Joseph Lamonaco was a World War II hero who fought in the second wave at Normandy Beach.[220]

Joseph worked as an electrician, and Grace stayed home to raise their family. They purchased a home on East Lincoln Avenue in town. Grace made sure that her husband had a hot meal on the table when he returned home after work. Grace would bear three children for Joseph: Philip, Diane and Deborah. Philip was born on Friday, January 21, 1949, and was baptized in

Standing proud. *Courtesy of Donna Lamonaco.*

Saint Andrews Church in Bayonne, where the family lived for a while. As Philip, Diane and Deborah grew, they became close. Philip (as they called him) played the big brother role to perfection. Deborah said, "He was the commensurate big brother." Joseph and Grace raised their children in an environment that was conducive to growth, prosperity and love—attributes that all three Lamonaco children have. It was also important to them that their children have strong senses of character, integrity and patriotism.[221]

The Lamonaco children attended the Robert Gordon Grammar School and the junior high school in town. Throughout his childhood, Lamonaco played in and about the local streets of Roselle Park. Down the road from his home is the intersection of Laurel and West Webster Avenues, where a park is named in honor of Lamonaco and his boyhood friend William Perry. (Perry was a New York/New Jersey Port Authority police officer who was killed in the line of duty.)[222]

In high school, Lamonaco was the average teenage boy with his sights on the opposite sex. Both sisters remember him having "a newfound concern on how he looked and dressed." Grace said that her son was always conscientious of what he wore. "Philip was a sharp dresser," said Diane. "He was particular about the way he wore his hair." During this time, Lamonaco enjoyed listening to music—not the popular rock sound of the time but rather Motown. "He would make fun of the fact that I liked the Beach Boys," recalled Diane.[223]

As a young teenager, Philip became involved in physical activity, with intense workouts consisting of weight training and jogging. "He loved to run, long before the running craze became popular," said Debbie. From an early age, Lamonaco was not satisfied with the status quo; he strove to be the best at what he did. It was a lifelong attribute, one that served him well as a Jersey trooper.[224]

By 1968, hostilities in Vietnam increased, highlighted by the Tet Offensive. The United States—which had been involved in the conflict in someway or the other since the 1950s—had begun combat operations in the early 1960s. "At a time when kids were going to college," said his sister, Debbie, "Philip enlisted!…He was that type of guy."[225]

Lamonaco became a United States Marine, probably because the marine motto "Semper Fidelis" ("Always Faithful" to the Corps and country) was similar to the Lamonaco credo of "Family and Country." Phil and his good friend, William Hinkle, enlisted together.[226]

Assigned to the Third Marine Division, Lamonaco was sent overseas and was involved in many combat operations, with the heaviest fighting taking place in the Quang Tri region. A steady stream of letters flowed back and forth across the ocean. Whether sitting in Rochelle Park or in a tent in Vietnam, each Lamonaco enjoyed reading his or her letter. "We would send Philip a basket every week," said his mother. "In each basket we put an assortment of his favorite foods, like tomato and crab sauce, with spaghetti… Philip had a large appetite." Debbie laughed. "Philip loved to eat." A shocking letter arrived one day from Philip asking his family to send COOL cigarettes. He had always been a health nut and "now was smoking." Apparently, the rigors of war caused him to venture into cigarette smoking. However, after a few letter exchanges, a postscript read, "Don't send any more 'COOL's.'" His nerves seemed to have settled down.[227]

Thirteen long months were spent by the man in combat. Afterward, he was greeted by a welcome home party. A lot had changed. The young kid who went off to war had come back a man. He was even stronger in his resolve and more disciplined than before.[228]

The motto of his Third Marine Division was "Fidelity, Honor and Value"; as a citizen, Lamonaco sought out an organization with a similar credo.[229]

The New Jersey State Police beckoned for Lamonaco and friend Bill Hinkle. The two had enlisted in the Marine Corps together and, on Friday, November 13, 1970, became troopers as graduating members of the eighty-

Donna and Phil. *Courtesy of Donna Lamonaco.*

third class. Trooper Lamonaco #2663 and Trooper Hinkle #2657 began their state police journey; Bill Hinkle's road was a long, industrious one that led to a retirement, whereas Lamonaco's was paved with tremendous success, unparallel notoriety and an enduring persistence to right the wrongs but was nonetheless a dead end.[230]

Lamonaco's career is legendary, lined with many criminal investigations. However, the most profound case was that of a broken windshield.[231]

Responding to a complaint of a broken windshield, the ambitious trooper in blue discovered a women who would capture his heart. Donna Benward was a year younger than Phil and was born and lived in Princeton, New Jersey. It wasn't obvious to Donna at first, but Lamonaco had a crush on her. He returned numerous times to the "scene of the crime" to follow up on the case with her. He even went so far as to leave his hat behind, to return once again. It wasn't until a friend of Donna told of Lamonaco's interest that he called her.[232]

Their first date was in April 1972 at a local disco called Hallabolloos. The evening started off poorly, recalled Donna, as Phil didn't want to dance, and they just sat talking. Afterward, they drove back to the barracks, where she parked her car. "Then," said Donna, "something special happened" when she put her hand out to say goodbye. Phil "grabbed it and said, 'My precious, you're coming with me'…and that was it." They drove all night and got to know each other. She got home at nearly 4:30 a.m. Donna said that she was "love struck."[233]

The remainder of the year saw the young couple going on day trips and going down the shore in Seaside, New Jersey. The two spent practically the whole summer on the Jersey sand.[234]

The year 1973 had the two falling in love, with talks of marriage. By March of the following year, Phil had bought an acre and a half of land in White Township and didn't tell Donna because he wanted to surprise her. He took her up to see it one cold day. Donna was not impressed, as it was a vacant lot with overgrown weeds and brush. It was hard for her to visualize a home being there. Then a light snow began to fall, covering the landscape. The bright sun's light reflected off the snow, painting a visual for her of what was to be.[235]

Construction began in September 1974, and Donna and Phil chose the church next door as the place of their wedding ceremony. Lamonaco was a Catholic but told his love that it didn't matter where he got married, so on March 15, 1975, the two were married in the United Methodist Church.[236]

The cost of their home drained all of the money for a honeymoon, so they spent time in their new house. Donna remembered talking with her sister and being told that they should go away for a least a weekend. Phil overheard the conversation and said, "Yeah, we're going to go right down that hall to the door on the left."[237]

In June 1976, Phil and Donna celebrated the birth of their daughter, Laura. A little over a year later, a son, Michael, was born. By 1977, Phil Lamonaco's reputation as a "Super Trooper" had been solidified. Everywhere he went, troopers knew who he was, and criminals avoided him like the plague. By 1978, Lamonaco was given a detective position that he reluctantly accepted, as he loved wearing the uniform.[238]

Lamonaco worked for a time as a detective and enjoyed the investigative work, but as time passed, his desire for what troopers call "the road" grew. He missed being a "Road Trooper" and finally asked to return to patrol. Many thought that he was crazy, but he was a man of his own convictions and was never swayed by others. The road was his calling, and he was going to return to it.[239]

Back in the French blue, in May 1978, Trooper John McCarthy #3265 graduated from the academy and was assigned to Phil as a trainee. Lamonaco was one of the best and most natural leaders the organization had in its ranks. McCarthy was in good hands.[240]

The following year witnessed Phil Lamonaco performing at a level few troopers could imagine; he was locking people up nearly every day. Thousands of dollars of illicit drugs and guns were being taken off the streets because of this one man. In the fall, he was nominated for the coveted "Trooper of the Year Award." The award had been instituted in 1968, and Lamonaco was to be the twelfth person to win the award.[241]

His success at his work was matched at home. He and Donna were doing an excellent job raising their family and creating memories for them that would last a lifetime. Donna and Phil would take the kids to the park, go on day trips or play in the backyard. Phil loved to cut firewood, with Donna helping by measuring each log. She had specific instructions—they were to be twenty-seven inches—which she marked with a screwdriver. Michael, always by his father's side, had his Fisher Price chainsaw, "helping Dad." The nights were filled with them all gathering in the family room, with Donna and Phil watching their children play. Oftentimes, Donna would read to them, with Phil listening eagerly while polishing his state police leather. On cold nights, Phil would throw logs into the fireplace, and they would sit by the warm fire.[242]

While driving down to Atlantic City on November 2, 1979, with Donna to attend the ceremony where he was to receive Trooper of the Year they heard over their AM radio the news of Joanne Chesimard, the killer of Werner Foerster, escaping from prison. Donna practically had to "hogtie him in the car" to prevent him from turning around to join in the search. Although he was a man of tremendous success, he was humbled by the honor that was bestowed on him that evening.[243]

The year 1980 was a challenging one for Lamonaco; he had to shoot and kill a deranged man who had pointed a shotgun muzzle at him. "He called me," said Donna. "I just wanted to let you know I'm ok…I was involved in a situation, and I wanted you to hear it from me before you hear it on the news." Lamonaco was a strong man and moved on. Then, in December, his good friend William Perry was killed in the line of duty. Perry's funeral was held during the Christmas holiday, and when Phil came home, he told Donna, "I hope I never have to attend anything like this again, never in my life." New Year's Eve was spent with Phil and Donna looking forward to a brighter year. Donna was due to give birth to their third child in February.[244]

After the birth of Sarah, the couple began planning a vacation. Six years had passed, and they had yet to go on a vacation. When summer arrived, Phil and Donna took a family vacation to Maine and enjoyed what was to be the first and only vacation as a family. [245]

Last family photo. *Courtesy of Donna Lamonaco.*

As Sarah grew, Phil "got her to say 'dah-dah,'" which thrilled him. Simply put, Lamonaco loved being a family man. The tough "super trooper" would allow little Laura to put curlers in his hair and could be seen sharing a candy cane with Sarah. Donna and the children made Lamonaco complete. Lamonaco was known for his strong sense of commitment to the troopers, but that paled in comparison to his family.

As Christmas 1981 neared, Phil and Donna were looking forward to it, as last year's holiday season had been darkened by the death of Bill Perry. Needless to say, the children were excited about their favorite time of year as well.[246]

December 1981 was an especially cold and a snow-filled month. The landscape was white with snow, and it was slated to be a "White Christmas." On the morning of December 21, Phil Lamonaco spent time with Donna and his children before heading to work. The temperature was cold, with a crisp feel in the air, as Phil walked to his car. Despite the cold weather, the sky was crystal blue, and the sun shone on the landscape, bringing back memories of the day Donna first gazed upon the vacant lot that was now their home.[247]

Hours later, history records the legendary trooper patrolling on Interstate 80 near the Knowlton rest area, which is at mile marker 4.0. Trooper Lamonaco spotted a vehicle with two white males at about four o'clock in the afternoon. Driving in that blue Chevy Nova were Thomas Manning and Richard Williams. Lamonaco could spot malevolent behavior a mile away, and Manning and Williams were masters at it. He stopped the vehicle at mile marker 3.6 on the westbound side of the highway.[248]

Manning and Williams were members of the underground criminal group known as the United Freedom Front (UFF). In fact, the UFF had been founded by Manning while he was in prison. From 1975 through 1984, the UFF pulled off several armed robberies and bombings in and around the northeast part of the United States. Moments after getting out of his car, a vicious firefight erupted, with the shots echoing across the Kittatinny Mountains. When the noise ended, Phil Lamonaco was found to have been mortally wounded, with a bullet finding a spot under his arm not protected by his vest.[249]

As Donna was baking cookies, she heard a knock at the door; from that moment on, her and her children's lives were changed forever.[250]

The funeral for Trooper Philip Lamonaco was attended by thousands of law enforcement officials from across the country. It is befitting that at the site where Lamonaco stopped Manning and Williams stand the Kittatinny Mountains; these large natural monuments are reminders of the towering man that was Philip Lamonaco.[251]

THE BLACK DRAGON

JOHN P. MCCARTHY #3265

John Patrick McCarthy was the second child to John and Dorothy McCarthy. The McCarthys, the surname originating from Belfast in Northern Ireland, married in April 1953. Dorothy (née Duetsch) was a German and Austrian woman of strong convictions. John and Dorothy lived in the "projects" on North Munn Avenue and South Orange Avenue in Newark. The projects are so coined because these dwellings were built by a government-funded "project" to house families of the military after World War II. Four children were born to the John and Dorothy: Michael, John, Brian and Noreen. Their son John, born on the Fourth of July in 1955, was a young trooper who gave his life protecting the citizens of New Jersey. It was a life that began with fireworks in the air, as Dorothy remembered hearing the Fourth of July celebrations from her hospital bed.[252]

Throughout the years, Newark has always had a place in the narrative of state police history. Troopers William Marshall #63 and Matthew McManus #144 were born here; John Ressler #494, James Scotland #594 and Joseph Walter #685 lived there; Robert Merenda #2393 played football on Newark's minor-league team; and the coldblooded killer of Warren Yenser #599 was captured on the city streets of Newark. It is fitting that John McCarthy's life began here, as he is part of the state police fabric.[253]

McCarthy's father, John (or Buster, as he was called) was a Korean War veteran and a decorated marine. After his service, Buster worked as a truck driver. Later on in life, he became a bartender and cab driver in town.

Buster "was easy to talk to, a great practical joker and well liked." However, it was Dorothy who did most of the child rearing. The McCarthy children credit their mother for their success. "Mom," said Bryan, "filled the emptiness with her love."[254]

Growing up, John and his siblings played games and roamed the city streets. Their games took on city parlance, such as "stoup ball" and "bases." Brian's fondest memories of him and John involved the two spending the whole day together building an igloo—only to knock it down fighting with each other. Dorothy said that her children were rambunctious: "We spent many hours at Saint Michaels Hospital" from roughhousing. Noreen credited her Catholic religion for their upbringing and said that it had a lasting impression on her brother John. McCarthy attended the Sacred Heart Grammar School in town and from an early age, said Noreen, "was conscientious and caring," especially toward his younger siblings. Every Sunday, Dorothy made sure that they went to church. John even served as an altar boy.[255]

Impromptu photo. *Courtesy of the McCarthy family.*

All four McCarthy children were agile, but Brian and John were the most athletic. They were avid wrestlers and runners. The running prepared them for wrestling season.[256]

After Sacred Heart, John McCarthy went to Seton Hall Prep High School and excelled in wrestling and cross-country. His high school senior year was highlighted by an upset victory over the Prep State champs in which John won in a decisive victory that brought the spectators out of their seats.[257]

As a high schooler, McCarthy was industrial. During this period, he worked several jobs. The most demanding of these was delivering bagels; John would wake up on weekends at four o'clock in the morning to begin his job. Sometimes he even delivered bagels before heading to school.[258]

High school proved to be a rewarding time for McCarthy. The most rewarding of all was meeting Nona Schuessler. Nona was a blond-haired beauty whom McCarthy bumped into through a mutual friend. Interestingly, that friend was Nona's date. "I remember we went out, and it was the first time I got to know John…my boyfriend wanted him to drink, and John refused." The young teenager "was struck with John's gentle yet resolute firmness and confidence." This is a testament to the young man's character. McCarthy had grown to be an attractive kid who stood nearly six feet tall and had curly blond hair, blues eyes and a toned body; presumably it wasn't just McCarthy's deportment that caught Nona's eye.[259]

It wasn't long before John was "gaga over Nona," said Brian. Nona occupied McCarthy's every thought. They became inseparable. Theirs was a high school courtship for the record books.[260]

Another father figure in John's life came by way of his soon-to-be father-in-law, William Schuessler. Now eighteen, it was legal for John to enter a bar, so he had the opportunity to get to spend more time with his father, who was bartending. Buster enjoyed seeing his son more, and their relationship was more friendship than father and son. At the same time, William Schuessler became a mentor to John. Schuessler was a retired Newark police officer whose influence over McCarthy turned out to be profound. Schuessler owned a bar called The Barge on Doremus Avenue in Port Newark, and John went to work there. McCarthy would listen intently to Schuessler's police stories. Nona said that her father told John, "You want to be the best, and the New Jersey State Police are the best." The die was cast, and the Irish kid from Newark set his sights on the elite organization.[261]

After high school, McCarthy worked as a delivery driver and as a bartender at the Half-Time/Time Out Emporium in Bloomfield.[262]

At the age of twenty-one, John and Nona began planning their wedding. By now John was living on his own in an apartment on Madison Avenue in Irvington, a place that Nona called the "Mancave."[263]

McCarthy had taken the state police test but had stalled at the interview phase when he was told that he was "not mature enough yet" and to "try again."[264]

History records John McCarthy as a member of the 93B class (interestingly, the only time classes were by "A" and "B" designations). While attending the academy, John and Nona married on his weekend leave. The date was Saturday, January 28, 1978, and the service was held in the Chapel of the Immaculate Conception on the campus of Seton Hall University in South Orange, New Jersey. John's pastor, Monsignor Kelly, performed the service. McCarthy and Kelly's friendship dated back to his high school days, and Noreen said that it was common for John to have connections from all periods of his life. "When

Mom and son. *Courtesy of the McCarthy family.*

John liked and respected someone, he liked them forever." The following Monday, McCarthy returned to the academy and changed his marital status. Interestingly, John listed his brother, Michael, as the person to be notified in case of an emergency.[265]

On April 21, 1978, John Patrick McCarthy graduated in a ceremony at the Sea Girt academy. Family and friends gathered in the National Guard Armory to watch as the members of the 93B class were ushered in military formation, shuffling their feet in cadence. It appeared that everyone was in awe as these impressive figures marched into view. During the ceremony, John Patrick McCarthy was bestowed badge #3265.[266]

McCarthy was stationed at the Blairstown Station and was assigned Trooper Phil Lamonaco #2663, a legend in the ranks of the state police. Lamonaco trained McCarthy well, and the young trooper was inspired to follow in the impressive trooper's footsteps.[267]

An interesting story the McCarthys liked to tell is when John came face to face with a bat. The rookie trooper was on patrol with Trooper D.E. Rehrig #3053 when a call of a bat in a home came in. According to Dorothy, John told her, "They trapped the bat using a tennis racket." John laughed when telling his mom the story and said, "I didn't expect to go head on with a bat." The woman was so pleased with the two troopers' handling of the situation that she wrote a letter of appreciation that still sits in his museum file in West Trenton.[268]

In July 1978, Nona gave birth to their first child, daughter Sharon. John and Nona were living in the rural community of Newton in an apartment. After Blairstown, McCarthy was transferred to the old Washington Station, a station dedicated to Cornelius O'Donnell #367, who was murdered while stationed there. His tour here would last only eight months as he was soon shipped to the Newark Station in Troop D.[269]

On July 14, 1979, John McCarthy worked his first day out of the Newark Station. This station contrasted sharply with his last two. Instead of streets lined with trees, they were lined with light poles and guardrails. Because he was working down by the city, he and Nona moved back to Irvington, taking up residence in an apartment at 242 Lincoln Place. That December, Nona gave birth to a son they named after John.[270]

Trooper McCarthy was certainly instructed by Lamonaco on the dangers of being a state trooper; however, now McCarthy was patrolling a road that troopers called "the Big Road." Many others referred to it as

Noreen, Brian, John and Michael. *Courtesy of the McCarthy family.*

"the Black Dragon." Illicit drugs and guns are transported up and down this roadway on a regular basis. The sheer volume of traffic alone makes this assignment dangerous. McCarthy's first eighteen months at Newark were marked by exceptional productivity, gaining him a commendation for "Outstanding Performance."[271]

The dangers of the "Black Dragon" hit McCarthy like a sledgehammer on Thursday, January 29, 1981. The three-year tenured trooper stopped a car for a minor motor vehicle infraction, and it went downhill from there. The occupants, Lewis Walker and Trenton Donald Dukes, were low-level criminals who were transporting a considerable amount of contraband. It didn't take long before McCarthy realized that the two were up to no good, causing Dukes to physically attack McCarthy and try to take his gun. Fighting for his life on the side of this busy highway, McCarthy gained control and shot Dukes, mortally wounding him.[272]

A short time later, at the Newark Station, John called Nona at a friend's house, where she was having dinner. He wanted to let her know that he was ok before she heard of the shooting on the news. A lesser man may have crumbled after an ordeal like this, but not John. He was strong and resolute. John would have preferred to not have had to fire his weapon, but he also knew that it was Trenton Duke's choice, not his.[273]

As the twenty-six-year-old trooper was getting ready to celebrate Christmas with Nona and his children, news of his mentor Phil Lamonaco being gunned down left him beside himself. The only thing that brightened the Christmas morning was sharing the joy with Nona of watching his children enjoy the holiday.[274]

With only four years as a trooper, McCarthy saw more than a trooper with twice his tenure. Sadly, this remarkable career was cut short while rendering assistance at an accident.[275]

It was the evening of September 25, 1982, and John McCarthy and Trooper Larry McClain #3266 stopped to check on a vehicle on the southbound side of the western extension at milepost 113.1. There were two vehicles stopped at this location, one on the left shoulder and one on the right. The troop car was pulled behind the vehicle on the right shoulder, and Trooper McCarthy walked across the highway to check on the driver on the left shoulder. While doing so, John was struck and killed crossing the highway. Personnel Order No. 223 formally announced the sad news of John Patrick McCarthy's death.[276]

ONE HELL OF A STRONG MAN

LESTER A. PAGANO SR. #1177

Lester Pagano was a strong and tenacious man; to fully understand him, one must first understand his background. Born on Friday, June 20, 1930, to Girbert and Gladys Pagano, Lester was the last of three children. Girbert (Bert) and Clinton were two and four when Lester was born. Both Girbert and Gladys were rodeo riders—or, as they liked to call themselves, "horse people." In the early twentieth century, Wild West shows were extremely popular. It wasn't long before figures such as Wyatt Earp and Jesse James were riding through the West. For the senior population, the memory of the Old West was etched into their minds, and they would take their kids to these "Wild West" programs—one of the most famous being that of the Buffalo Bill and the Famous 101 Ranch Show out in Oklahoma. Gladys was one of the performers in these shows.[277]

Pagano's mother, Gladys DeVere Weedon, went by the stage name of "Dixie DeVere." Hanging on the wall of the home of Lester's brother, Clinton Pagano, is a panoramic photo of the old 101 ranch rodeo team taken in 1914, with his mother in it. Dixie was well known and respected and used to perform dangerous stunts on horseback. According to the famous Will Rogers, Dixie was a "great cowgirl rider." How Dixie met her future husband, Girbert, has been lost with the passing of time. Since Girbert, too, was a rodeo rider, it is safe to say that they met while performing together. Shortly after that panoramic picture was taken, the Buffalo Bill Cody Show and the 101 Ranch merged. It is said that the 101 Ranch was formed and owned by Dixie's relatives.[278]

In 1926, the two rodeo riders married; the couple would have three children: Girbert, Clinton and Lester. Girbert and Gladys were gainfully employed as rodeo riders, bringing in significant incomes. With this money, the two invested in several lucrative real estate transactions in Oklahoma.[279]

During the early years of the twentieth century, "Wild West" shows and vaudeville acts were extremely popular, but as the years progressed, they began to fade out. A new form of entertainment was getting a foothold in the entertainment industry. Motion picture production proved to gain traction and pushed the live acts out of business. One of the most

Lester Pagano. *Courtesy of Colonel Clinton Pagano.*

famous companies at the time was the Fox production company, which had operations in New Jersey and a production site in Englewood Cliffs. The Paganos happened to be living in Englewood Cliffs and managed to secure a contract with Fox. They would provide horses, props, equipment and riding skills for movie shoots. The couple managed this profitable business while raising three rambunctious boys.[280]

The Pagano business was so successful that the family wasn't affected by the Great Depression. However, a tragic accident would change the family forever.[281]

Rodeo riding is a dangerous occupation, and both Dixie and Girbert received their share of injuries throughout the years. Because of these dangers, Girbert was killed by a freak accident in 1931 when a horse kicked him in the head. At the time, his children were only five, three and one. During this period, Gladys adopted a "child off the streets": Philip Worshing. She had known Philip's father, who couldn't care for his son any longer, so she took him in. In spite of all this, Gladys Pagano was still able to maintain her business until another unfortunate event ruined her financially. While transporting several expensive horses, an accident killed several of the animals. Insurance wasn't a requirement, and she didn't have any. The common practice at the time was to let the client suffer the loss. This went against Gladys Pagano's grain, and so she made sure that her client received total compensation for the loss, at the expense of her total financial ruin.[282]

An old friend, Emil Wulster of Blairstown, New Jersey, talked Gladys into buying property in Blairstown, believing that she could make a living with a horse business there. With her four children, she moved into the farmhouse on Cedar Lake that had a large tract of property and a large barn. Gladys had hoped that things would turn around. "Piece by piece, everything went down financially" said Clinton Pagano. His mother was a proud women and found it hard to come to terms with the fact that she had made a terrible business move. Eventually, she had to sell everything. For a time, the Paganos moved from town to town "This was taking place right in the middle of the Depression," said Clinton. "It was a time when if there was food on the table you were doing fine." And his mother always made sure that food was there for her children.[283]

Eventually, Gladys obtained a job working at a hospital in New York, where her sister was working. This allowed for her to finally find a permanent place for them to live. They moved to Cliffside Park, New Jersey. Up until this time, they were moving every year.[284]

When 1940 arrived, World War II had been going on for sometime, with the United States keeping a watchful eye on activities. Roosevelt did all he could to adhere to the isolationist ideology that Washington had alluded to in his farewell address—an ideology that the United States had held for more than a century. However, once we were attacked at Pearl Harbor, everything changed. Droves of citizens rose to the occasion and enlisted in the military. It was a time of unparalleled patriotism. The Paganos were as patriotic as any family. Gladys had instilled in her children strength of character, discipline, determination and family values. Clinton Pagano said that his mother "was a strong woman." Her boys were strong as well. Philip, although adopted, was very much a Pagano—headstrong and tough, he, like his adoptive mother, believed that "when your country needs you, you don't wait for them to come get you; you go." Philip enlisted in the Marine Corps.[285]

One morning, at about 3:00 a.m., the doorbell rang. It was a Western Union man with a letter from the United States Marine Corps advising of Philip's death. What a terrible way of hearing of your son's death. Where he had been killed or how were facts not included in the letter. It was devastating news, and then her son Bert enlisted without telling anyone. He simply went off, leaving the family for a time to wonder where he was. This left her with Clinton and Lester. The troubles that the Pagano family endured were difficult but brought them together. Clinton Pagano called this his "formative years." Toward the close of the war, Clinton joined the United States Army and went to the Far East. There Clinton had some medical problems and ended up in Fort Dix, New Jersey, at Chilton General Hospital. Lester, still in high school, would trek all the way down to visit his brother. Transportation wasn't what it is today. He had to take a bus into New York and then a bus to Trenton and finally a train to Fort Dix. The closeness that the two shared is evident in the lengths Lester took to see his brother. "He never came without some tale about the troopers," Clinton fondly remembered. Troopers had always been a presence in the Blairstown area when the Pagano brothers were small. The boys were in awe of those imposing figures in French blue. In Englewood Cliffs, troopers were also active and very much a presence. As such, the state police left a lasting impression on the Pagano children. Clinton said that "it was ingrained in my head, and Lester and Bert." It was a single goal shared by three. The Pagano boys were "emotionally joined at the hip." Saying that they were close is an understatement.[286]

After Lester Pagano graduated Cliffside Park High School, he followed in his three brothers' footsteps and joined the military. A testament to their sense of leadership and individuality, each went their own patriotic way toward their military endeavors. Clinton joined the United States Air Force. He began with the organization in 1948 and served in Texas until 1949.

Clinton Pagano had applied to the state police and was rejected because he was told that he wasn't a "wartime veteran." The outfit—or, more likely, the person in charge of recruitment at that time—made a mistake in disqualifying him under those conditions. In light of the state police's rejection, Clinton Pagano and Lester were under the impression that they needed to be war veterans to be troopers. So, after completing his tour with the air force in 1950, Lester, along with Clinton and three other friends, went down and enlisted in the Marine Corps. The Korean war was underway in June and serving during this period would make them eligible to become troopers. However, by the time the state police rectified the problem, it was too late. Clinton Pagano was now a marine.[287]

As a marine, Lester worked as a military policeman. It was a job that he thoroughly enjoyed and would be the foundation for what was to come.[288]

Of the Pagano boys, Clinton was the first to become a trooper, with Lester following a year later in December 1952 from the forty-second class. Lester's first assignment came at the old Somerville Barracks, a place rich in state police history that dates back to the first murder of a Jersey trooper when Bob Coyle #238 was killed. June 1952 saw Lester working out of the Pompton Lakes Barracks for a brief tour before being transferred to the Flemington Barracks. Christmas 1954 had a special feeling in the air as the two trooper Pagano boys were anticipating their older brother Bert's state police graduation.[289]

The year 1955 saw all three Paganos donning the French Blue uniform. All three men would experience their share of danger. One incident deeply upset Lester and Clinton: Bert had been handling a bar dispute at a place called Aunt Kate's Tavern in Netcong and was stabbed with a knife, landing him on a ventilator for a period of time. The dangers of the job were to become well known to the Pagano boys.

The opening month of 1956 witnessed Lester Pagano being transferred to his old stomping grounds in Warren County. "Up until that point, like all troopers, we had been all over God's creations. But when Lester got back to Blairstown, he got back to home territory," said Clinton Pagano. As children, the Pagano boys dreamed of being troopers—that dream had become reality. Blairstown Station provided police services to most of the towns in the area; basically, troopers were the law. Today, this still holds true. Lester loved police work, and "above anything else," said Clinton, "my brother was a worker. He wouldn't let any grass grow under his feet."[290]

By 1959, Lester had been married, divorced and remarried. He had four children—Lester Jr., Fern Louise, David and Michael—from his first marriage and a daughter, Barbara, from his marriage to his second wife, Betty.[291]

Then, an event in 1959 put an indelible mark on the Pagano family. On November 25, a well-known and well-loved store owner named Lester Silverman was brutally murdered on Main Street in Blairstown. The crime scene sent shivers down the spines of the citizenry. Silverman's dry goods store had been in the family for years and dated back to the nineteenth century. "We used to call him [Silverman] 'Abbie,'" said Clinton. This horrid crime left every citizen feeling vulnerable.[292]

The main suspect in the case was a man named Stanley Marrs. Like Silverman, Marrs was a lifelong resident. He, too, was well known, but for his hostility rather than for his benevolence. People in town called Marrs "Batman"—not because of heroics but because of the beating he gave his girlfriend and three others with a bat.[293]

Lester Pagano and Trooper James Suydam #1383 arrived on the scene to investigate the crime. At the time of their arrival, Silverman was still alive. The brutal beating Silverman took led the two troopers to believe that Marrs was their primary suspect. Word on the street was that Marrs was hanging his hat at a local hotel in Johnsonburg, an old stagecoach and railroad town that is actually part of Frelinghuysen Township and is virtually in the middle of nowhere. To this day, this community looks like a place out of an old TV western.[294]

Driving to this isolated community, the troopers traveled the rural roads over the Paulins Kill River, as well as the Silver Lake and Dark Moon Roads. The village has a handful of buildings, and the Johnsonburg Inn is easy to spot when entering town. It is a three-story building with the first and second floor sporting a wooden deck. The building dates back to the 1800s and has wooden rails that were once used by visitors to tie up their horses. Once a beautiful inn, it was now an inexpensive refuge for local riffraff. A large stairway and a large rustic bar could be seen as the two troopers entered and walked up to the apartment where Marrs was staying. The door was open, so the troopers took some liberties and entered. Inside the room, they found a bloodstained shirt. By this time, they had learned of Silverman's death and Suydam left to return to the crime scene for a more detailed investigation. Pagano remained behind, awaiting Marrs's return. Clinton Pagano remembered Stanley Marrs well: "Marrs was a bodybuilder. He was called the Batman and was a tremendous, tremendously aggressive, abusive kind of guy…everybody in that territory knew Stanley Marrs." What was to follow should have been expected.[295]

Marrs came into the room with his coat over his arms, and when Pagano spotted him, he realized that Marrs was hiding a handgun. Next "they went hand to hand," recalled Clint Pagano. "Lester was in plainclothes, but Marrs knew him, and he knew Marrs." Recalling the event later, Lester couldn't remember when he was first shot. It was either in the room or in the area immediately outside the room. The bullet entered Pagano's body under his heart and ricocheted off a bone, traveling into the upper neck and settling in Pagano's spinal cord. A lesser man would have fallen immediately. Holding on to Marrs, the two men fell head over heels down the large staircase to the first floor. Marrs then fled out the door, but not without first being shot by Pagano, who shot over his head as Marrs fled (all three Pagano boy's were taught to "point and shoot" by their mother). Then, virtually paralyzed, Lester crawled on his elbows out the front door,

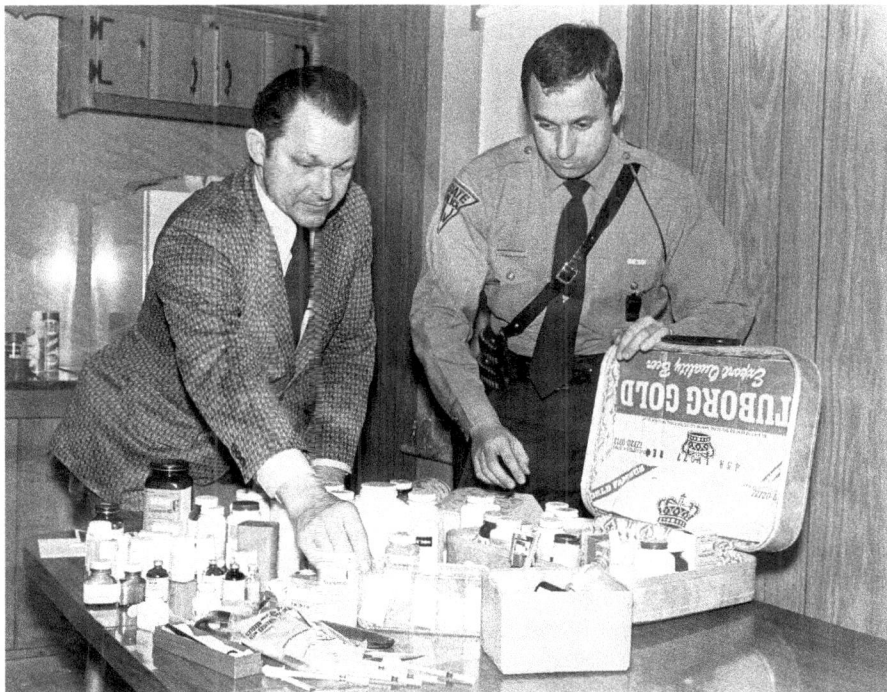

Lester and Philip Lamonaco (proceeds from a drug bust). *Courtesy of Colonel Clinton Pagano.*

where, as Clinton Pagano tells the story, "Lester shot Marrs, but Marrs wasn't able to put another bullet into Lester."[296]

Arriving troopers found Pagano and Marrs lying helpless on the street. Both were rushed to the hospital—with Pagano being the more seriously injured, he was taken to the Newton Hospital, whereas Marrs was brought to Warren Hospital in Phillipsburg, Pennsylvania.[297]

For the next two years, Lester Pagano lay motionless, paralyzed from the neck down. Through conventional therapy from Dr. Kessler and homeopathic therapy administered at advice of Pagano's mother, Lester slowly regained movement and control of his body. It is a testament to the man that he was. In order to fight and regain control of his functions, Lester Pagano refused medication: "If I can't feel the pain, I can't return my body to normal." Doctors wanted to remove the bullet in his spine, but there was a risk of permanent paralysis, so Pagano refused the procedure. "Screw it," Lester said. His brother remembered, "That was his attitude. Right up until the day of his death, when I was superintendent, whatever he said, that's the way it went." It was Lester's life, his family and his job. Clinton Pagano said, "I never doubted him, but I wasn't happy about it as a brother."[298]

Although Pagano had defied the odds and had returned to being able to walk, his recovery process took more than a decade. While Marrs sat behind bars, Pagano was a prisoner of his injury. For his heroic actions on that November day, Pagano was awarded the highest honor that a trooper can achieve: the Distinguished Service Medal. In the forty years of the outfit, only thirteen troopers received this honor.[299]

When the day finally came that Pagano returned to work, he arrived at the Blairstown Station and received a round of applause from troopers. Then Pagano went to walk into the station, which was located on the second floor. Many extended a helping hand, but this wasn't met well by Pagano. Clinton Pagano mentioned what happened next. "My brother said, 'I'm coming up myself. If I can't rehabilitate myself, or my reputation, I'm the local cripple,' His words, not mine," said the former superintendant. Clinton laughed. "That was his attitude."[300]

The next decade witnessed Lester Pagano struggling with his injuries. That bullet caused many high fevers. At one point, a captain went to great lengths to get Pagano forcefully retired through a medical retirement. If not for the intervention of the then handicapped attorney general Arthurs J. Sills, Pagano would have been discharged from the organization. "I remember," said Clinton Pagano, "a guy who used to work with me fell off a motorcycle, broke his ankle and [then it was,] 'Get out of here; we don't need you anymore!' That was the way the organization worked." As superintendant, Clinton Pagano did a lot to change that, but as they say, that is another story. There wasn't a doubt from Lester or his brothers that he would regain control of his health. "They don't understand the logic. But they didn't grow up the way we did. They didn't have the background that we had. I've seen my mother dragged by a horse a long distance, banging her head, but she would do her own thing and get up on the horse again." To put it simpler, "Lester could get himself going if he got at it." The only thing he needed was time. Arthur Sills gave him the time he needed.[301]

The next decade saw improvement physically, and with the love and caring of his beloved wife, Betty, and his children (Lester, Fern, Louise, David, Michael and Barbara), he carried on. He had hobbies that he enjoyed such as woodworking, hunting and fishing. Many friends of his have birdhouses or some other knickknack made at the hands of Lester. Performing this craft was mentally therapeutic for him.[302]

A series of promotions soon followed; he was designated a detective in January 1977, made detective sergeant a year and a half later and in late 1979 was promoted to detective sergeant first class and was put in charge of the Criminal Investigation Section at Totowa Headquarters. Then, in July 1981, Pagano was assigned to Greystone State Hospital as chief of security. There he would rise to the rank of lieutenant.[303]

In December 1981, State Trooper Phil Lamonaco was murdered, which launched a nationwide manhunt for the killers. Lester and Clint Pagano were good friends of Lamonaco's and took his death personally. The night of the murder, a command post was set up, with Colonel Clinton Pagano at the site. "I went to our command post…between Blairstown and Columbia. I looked, there was my brother. I said to him, 'What the hell are you doing here?' He said, 'I just got transferred.'" Clinton Pagano laughed while telling the story. "I said, 'Who transferred you?' He said, 'I transferred myself.' I tell you, my brother had more balls than you can imagine." The die was cast. Lester was in charge.[304]

With his deteriorating health and the strains of the investigation, it was too much for him to handle. Quite simply, he was exhausted and worked himself too hard. Colonel Pagano believed this to be true. "As time was going by, him pushing the way he was, his body began to deteriorate." Even so, he was able to continue, but not without a cost. "His bone structure was going bad," said his brother "One day, [Lester] called and said, 'Goddamn, I think I have a broken leg.' I asked, 'How did you break your leg?' Lester replied, 'I don't know but it won't make a difference.'" And it didn't. The leg would eventually have to be amputated, with Lester returning to work with a wooden leg. "Lester was always a shining example of what a trooper ought to be," says his brother Clinton. Strong, determined and steadfast, Lester Pagano was one of the best the outfit had. In a twist of fate, a dark rainy day in July 1983 did what Marrs's bullet couldn't do.[305]

The date was Tuesday, July 19. Lester Pagano was working out of Troop B headquarters following up loose ends on the Lamonaco investigation. Afterward, he left and began a long journey back to the Knowlton Command Post in Warren County. The long trip was exacerbated by rain. The pinging of rain on the roof and the methodical sound of the windshield wipers provided an ambience for reflection as Pagano traveled the I-80 corridor. Possibly he thought of his wife and kids or his three beautiful grandchildren. Maybe he pondered the investigation and thought of his old friend Phil Lamonaco. Regardless of his thoughts, something terrible happened. Pagano ran off the road and struck a concrete bridge abutment, and his car flipped and fell onto the road below the interstate. The accident occurred at milepost 33.6. Investigators believe that Pagano's car began to hydroplane due to water puddles in the grooves of the road.[306]

On Friday, July 22, Lester Pagano was laid to rest at Cedar Ridge Cemetery in Blairstown. Lester Pagano was fifty-three years old. A former partner of Pagano's named Thomas Evans #2331 penned a tribute called "Hero" for his friend:

> *I asked him* [Lester] *once why he's still doing police work. We were sitting in a cold car in front of a bank, hoping that the tip we had was good and that several well-armed men would attempt to hold this bank up. It was in these moments that I began to understand DSG Pagano. He just looked at me and asked why I was there. You see, Lester doesn't think he is different. He knows that he limps, he knows that he deals with more pain than most people, but he has come to grips with these facts and you can sometimes see in his eyes that he wonders why men ask such foolish questions…Hero, the word was coined on the strength of men like our departed friend.*[307]

ALWAYS A SMILE ON HIS FACE

EDWARD R. ERRICKSON #3875

Edward Raymond Errickson was born on July 31, 1937, to Leo and Christine Errickson. Both Leo and Christine were of Swedish roots. The couple lived in the Cumberland County town of Millville, where they raised their six children: Isabelle, Letitia, Carol, Leo, Gary and Edward. Leo supported his family by working for the Millville City and Streets Department. The Erricksons sent their children through the public school system, and this is where Edward received his education. As a child, Eddie enjoyed sports and was athletic and showed skills in a variety of physical activities.[308]

By the time Edward Errickson entered high school, his interested in sports continued. His wife Rita (née Smith) said that her husband was good at "anything in the sports line." Rita was a few years behind Edward in high school but remembered that they used to see each other every Saturday night at the YMCA dances. In school, friends used to call him "Ecky" rather than Ed or Edward. Ecky was a social kid who enjoyed spending time with his friends. High school was a rewarding time for the young man. One day, he and his brother, along with friends, went to Coney Island, where Eddie decided to get a tattoo. A mishap left a lasting mark on the young man. Errickson asked for his nickname to be displayed proudly on his body. The tattoo artist misspelled the name, and forever more Errickson bore the name "Esky" on his body.

At his high school graduation in June 1956, Errickson stood five feet eleven and had a medium build, with a smile that lit up his face. He began to entertain

Airman second class. *Courtesy of Rita Errickson.*

thoughts of military service. In the fall, the blue-eyed brown-haired Errickson enlisted in the United States Air Force. While in the service, his relationship with Rita blossomed, and the two started discussing getting married. That moment came on Saturday, August 30, 1958. Afterward, Rita moved in with her husband on the military base in Homestead, Florida. Errickson became a jet mechanic and remained in that capacity throughout his tenure in the air force. When one looks at his military photo, you could see that the young serviceman was extremely happy and proud. His service had been a rewarding experience, and he was embarking on a long and happy life with Rita. He was honorably discharged in January 1961 with the rank of airman second class.[309]

Errickson and Rita moved into an apartment in Millville, and he began working as a mold maker for Maul Bros., a pharmaceutical company. The couple had three children: Linda, Michael and Lisa. In January 1967, he and Rita were financially secure and purchased a house of their own. The couple enjoyed their life together and watching their children grow. After working as a mold maker for several years, Errickson applied to the New Jersey Highway Patrol Bureau. This organization (now defunct) was responsible for vehicle inspections. Officers would patrol the highways inspecting cars or were assigned at inspection stations. Errickson was accepted into training and successfully graduated from the eleventh motor vehicle class in March 1965.[310]

Highway Patrol Officer Errickson #9363 worked in and around the southern and central portion of the state. Throughout his tenure with the organization, he worked out of Vineland and Atlantic City. Edward Errickson worked with Highway Patrol for eighteen years, and in that time the New Jersey State Police came to oversee that organization. As time progressed, the state police moved closer to absorbing the officers of Highway Patrol into its ranks.[311]

Family photo. *Courtesy of Rita Errickson.*

As the Errickson children grew, Rita and Edward became active in their children's lives. Edward coached on the pigtail and ponytail leagues. He enjoyed sports and loved being a part of his children's athletic activities. The family used to vacation at Sea Isle in New Jersey and twice went to Disney World in Florida. For Edward and Rita, the most enjoyment came with staying home as a family. Rita remembered that her husband had a missing tooth that was replaced by a single tooth denture. Every now and again, he

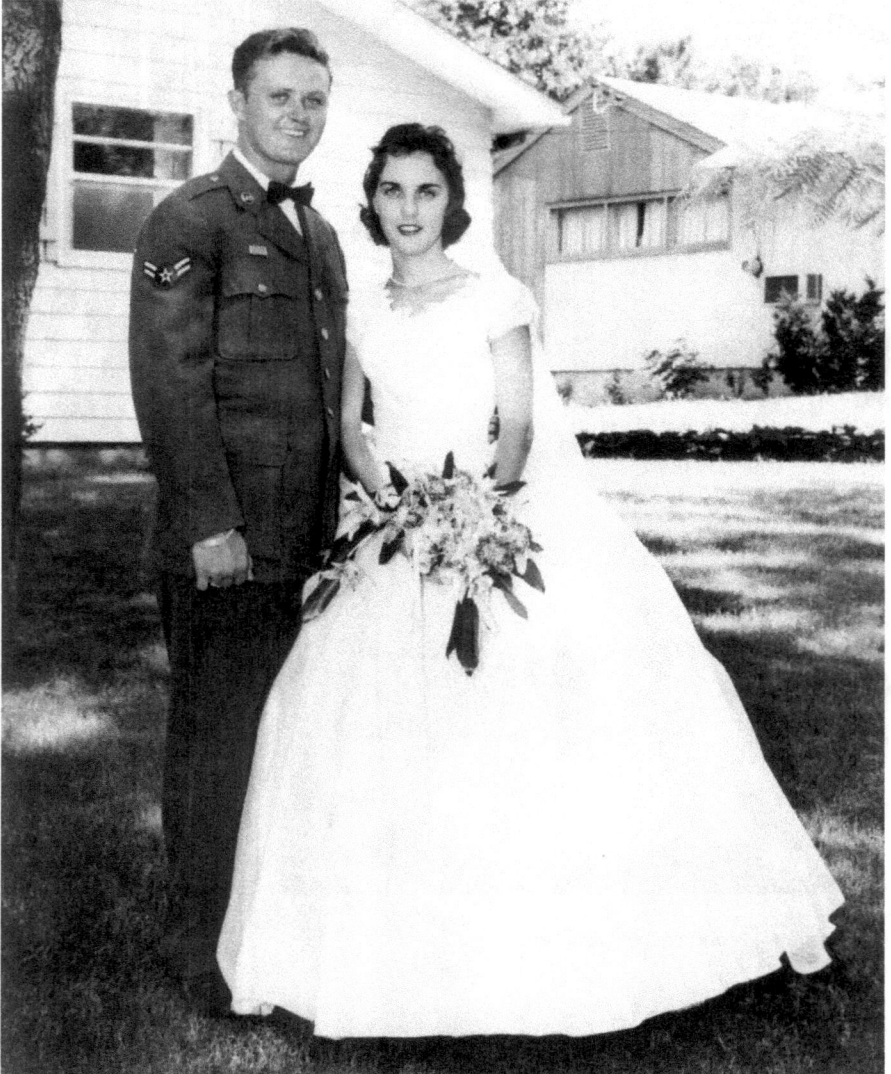

Newlyweds. *Courtesy of Rita Errickson.*

would let it fall out to get amusement out of his children. Errickson always had a smile on his face and was very easy to get along with. He was especially kind to Rita and the kids. He also used to like curling his lip in the Elvis fashion to get a laugh out of people. Eddie also enjoyed quiet days at home watching the Phillies. From time to time, he liked to get out and play golf. But most of all, it was spending time with his children and wife. Whether coaching or at home all together, it was all about his family. To this day, "The kids never forgot the day he dropped the family dinner, a casserole, all over the patio." Rita didn't find it funny at the time, "but the kids thought it was hysterical, and so do I now," recalled Rita.

After working nearly nineteen years with Highway Patrol, the state police were about to officially absorb the officers into its ranks. It was January 1984, and the paperwork for that transition had already been approved by the attorney general's office. With days away from that transition, Officer Errickson was driving his patrol vehicle in heavy fog on State Highway 47. The date was Tuesday, January 10, 1984, and it was a cold morning, with fog settling down on the roadways, making for difficult driving conditions. Errickson was traveling southbound. "I was doing around 30," Errickson told authorities, "when I started to slide apparently hit a patch of ice." The veteran officer tried to maintain control of his vehicle. "I attempted to straighten the vehicle out but was unable to." Heading northbound toward Errickson was William Peter of Heislerville, New Jersey. "I saw the car coming south," Peter said. "I pulled towards the shoulder," but Errickson's car slid completely sideways, and Peter's car t-boned the driver's side of the patrol car. "I was just coming out of the curve," Errickson said. "The last thing I recall was the impact on my side." The trauma from the collision caused extensive internal damage to the father of three. While Errickson was struggling for his life, the personnel order from the state police came out making Edward Errickson a Jersey trooper with badge #3875. Errickson always enjoyed the job he was doing with Highway Patrol, and it is sad that the man never got to be part of the full transition into the ranks of the state police. It was a challenging period for the organization, and Errickson would have excelled in his new capacity as a trooper.

Trooper Errickson died on January 25 at Millville Hospital from his internal injuries sustained on that foggy Tuesday morning.[312]

TROOPER DOWN

CARLOS M. NEGRON #3656

The story of Carlos Manuel Negron is one of a young inner city youth rising above the difficulties that life had to offer and achieving his goal of becoming a New Jersey State Trooper.[313]

Carlos Negron was born on October 2, 1954, in Santurce, Puerto Rico, to Daniel and Julia (née Cadiz) Negron. Carlos was the second of ten children, and the couple moved to the continental United States in 1956, to the urban community of Trenton, New Jersey. Daniel and Julia had little money but provided as best they could. They were devout Catholics and sent their children to Saint Mary's Cathedral Grammar School in Trenton. At school, Carlos enjoyed school activities, became active in the church and was an altar boy. The youth seemed to enjoy church and spending time in and around the parish. Carlos had a strong interest in learning about God.[314]

Carlos was an energetic young man who began working at age twelve, delivering papers for the *Trentonian* newspaper in town. At a young age, Carlos realized that he needed to work hard to make money and rise above the financial struggles that he saw with his parents and within his neighborhood. He wanted to make something of himself and help his parents with the extra money he brought in. Carlos Negron had a caring nature about him and was extremely close to his parents and his siblings (Daniel Jr., Maria, Jennie, Richard, Eddie, Enrique, Michael, David and Robert.). Their parents taught each the value of family. For young Carlos, he was blessed with an industrious nature and likeability. While delivering papers, his clients became fond of him and often paid him for doing various jobs around the neighborhood. Before long, Carlos was the handy kid on the block and could even be seen making grocery pickups for the elderly, who would pay him to get their goods.[315]

In addition to his after-school paid activities, Carlos enjoyed a healthy sports program in school. At home, he and his siblings played basketball, spending fun hours together. Carlos was an athletic kid who also enjoyed football and swimming. He also used to exercise regularly, which included an intense cardio program centered on running. Although Daniel and Julia had little money, they made sure that their children had some fringe benefits, such as buying them a pool table. Many hours were spent by the Negron children in their basement playing pool together. All became good players, with their games becoming competitive and challenging. Carlos's sister Jennie remembered the hot summer nights without air conditioning. Daniel and Julia couldn't afford to take their children on long vacations, so they would do day trips. One of the locations was the Jamesburg Beach in New Jersey. "We were lucky if our parents could afford to take us to the beach

Left to right: Carlos, Richard and Daniel Jr., circa 1961. *Courtesy of the Negron family.*

three times during the summer," Jennie once wrote. Despite their financial setbacks, the Negrons had a nice home life. They had droves of friends and used to have holiday parties.[316]

As a teenager, Carlos attended the Cathedral High School for three years and then the Notre Dame High School in Lawrenceville, New Jersey, when Cathedral closed down. There he enjoyed an active life both in school and out. At night, he would work as a busboy for the Holiday Inn in Trenton. Carlos's work had partially helped to pay for his attendance at Saint Mary's, and he continued to help his parents pay for his education while in high school. Carlos understood that he had to work hard and get an education to break the hold that the inner city held on him and his family. The Negrons lived in a drug-infested neighborhood. However, Carlos knew to stay away from the bad elements. He wanted to make something of his life, and his desire to be a trooper helped him to avoid trouble.[317]

In June 1973, Carlos graduated high school and entered the College of New Jersey. There he studied criminal justice and became active in the Latino student organization, serving as a treasurer and rising to become its president.[318]

In 1980, Carlos Negron tried out and was accepted into training for the state police. However, he wasn't as physically fit as needed for the strenuous academy training and dropped out. He was beside himself. He had always wanted to be a trooper and now had failed in this endeavor. But like he had proven as a child in a difficult environment, he was capable of rising above. So he joined the United States Marine Corps Reserve to condition himself for the rigors of state police academy training.[319]

Carlos Manuel Negron did fulfill his boyhood dream to become a New Jersey state trooper in February 1982 as a graduating member of the ninety-eighth class.

Somewhere in time, Carlos met a young women named Aida Maldonado and fell in love. The two married and took up residence in Trenton. During the first year with the organization, Carlos patrolled out of Troop C. His first station was Hopewell, and then he was moved to Fort Dix. In May 1983, Carlos and Aida had their first child together, a son they named Carlos Manuel. Then on August 6, 1983, Trooper Negron was transferred to Troop D and assigned to the New Brunswick Station.[320]

Ten years had passed since troopers at the New Brunswick Station had encountered members of the Black Liberation Army (BLA). In that time, increased awareness and improved officer survival training had taken place within the organization. When Trooper Negron reported to his first

High school photo. *Courtesy of the Negron family.*

day of work here, he was reminded of the deadly encounter by seeing a picture of Werner Foerster #2608 hanging on the wall. The next nine months witnessed Negron working the central portion of the turnpike and spending quality time on his days off with Aida and young Carlos. Then came Monday, May 7, 1984, and state records have Carlos Negron pulling up to a 1976 blue Ford van to render assistance northbound at milepost 66.7 in East Windsor Township. As the young trooper opened the door to troop car 823, he was about to encounter two hardened criminals.

Lenel Hutchinson, age thirty-nine, had an extensive criminal record for armed robberies. James Daniels, age forty-three, had shot to death a man in Queens County, New York, in 1963 and was sentenced to fifty years in prison. In 1976, after only serving twelve years, he was paroled. Daniels was a member of the BLA and was wanted by authorities as a suspect in several murders. Now, as the two men stood by their disabled vehicle, a Jersey trooper was approaching. Daniels was not going to take any chances. He took out his 9mm Browning high-powered semiautomatic handgun and opened fire on Negron as he walked. Unfortunately, Negron didn't have on a bulletproof vest, and the wounds he received became fatal.[321]

Daniels and Hutchinson fled on foot across open fields and came upon a landscaping company, where they bound and gagged three men and stole their business van. A short while later, Trooper Thomas Suscewiez #3460 spotted the two suspects in the van, and a high-speed chase got underway. The state police radio lit up with the sounds of sirens blaring and the tire streaks of a high-speed vehicle. With speeds over one hundred miles per hour, Trooper Suscewiez chased the vehicle on State Highway 33. Hutchinson was driving the van and did all he could to lose the determined trooper and other police cars on his tail. At milepost 18.2 on SH 33, Hutchinson lost control and struck a utility pole, splitting his van in two. The crash was a gory scene of twisted metal and body parts. For

"Just Married." *Courtesy of the Negron family.*

Daniels and Hutchinson, justice was served immediately for the killing of a Jersey trooper.[322]

Carlos Manuel Negron is fondly remembered by the residents of Trenton and nearby Hamilton, especially the Hispanic community there. Carlos was a shining example of how an inner city kid rose above the difficulties of urban life and made something of himself. Today, a park at the corner of Calhoun and Passaic Streets in Trenton bears his name.

A WEDDING AND A FUNERAL

WILLIAM L. CARROLL JR. #3296

Bill Carroll was a towering man. He was strong, courageous and loving—in essence, a gentle giant. This is his story, which began on Saturday, June 25, 1955, in New Brunswick, New Jersey. The first of six children, Carroll's father, William, was born in 1935 in Brooklyn, New York, and was a second-generation Ukrainian. The surname Carroll was actually spelled as Karol; however, for American ease, it was changed to the present spelling. The elder Carroll grew up in Brooklyn and moved as an adult to New Jersey, where he met his wife Nancy (née Delanoy) in New Brunswick. Nancy was of Irish and German descent. The couple lived in a public housing apartment at 102 Wright Place in New Brunswick. There, with these humble beginnings, William Lawrence Carroll Jr. was raised.[323]

That nice-sized apartment eventually grew small with the onset of Carroll's siblings: Jay, David, Judy, Joy and Christopher. Their father worked as the superintendent of grounds at Saint Peter's Cemetery in town, and Nancy was a secretary there. All of the Carroll children were put through the public school system, with William beginning his education at the McKinley Grammar School on Van Dyke Avenue in the fall of 1960. However, one year later, Carroll was sent to Saint Peter's Grammar School.[324]

Carroll's years in school were marked by academic success and impressive sports performances, despite his lesser record of attendance. In his sophomore year alone, Carroll was absent forty-five times. By the time the brown-haired and brown-eyed Carroll was fifteen, he stood nearly six

William Carroll Jr. #3296. *Courtesy of Christopher Carroll.*

feet tall and had a large muscular frame. At his graduation, he weighed 225 pounds of sheer muscle. Needless to say, when his high school years ended, Carroll had amounted an impressive football record. Moreover, his sports activities also included bowling, baseball, weightlifting, basketball and cross-country track. Chris Carroll said that Bill didn't realize his own strength: "He would put me behind the plate and throw the ball at me…I can still feel the pain."[325]

The summer after graduating high school, Bill Carroll began working for a family friend as a mason. Now in his eighteenth year of life, Carroll tried to parlay his baseball skills into a profession, unsuccessfully trying out for the Cincinnati Reds. After working three years as a mason, Carroll took a night job to earn extra income. He bounced at a local establishment called the Red Fox Inn. As a bouncer, few challenged him, and those who did regretted doing so.[326]

By this time, Carroll was an impressive figure of sheer size and strength. Moreover, he was a practitioner of martial arts and a holder of a fourth-degree black belt. "He would hit the walls in the house," said Chris, "sometimes penetrating…and would throw punches landing an inch away from your face." His sibling also remembered that Bill enjoyed "busting chops" and "joking around." There existed a large gap in years between the two, but Chris remembered the softer and warmer side to his brother well. He "would always go out of his way to help you…He was my big brother…I remember he got a brand-new Cougar and let me take it to my junior prom." Big Bill Carroll loved his siblings and showed them by taking care of them. Burning the candles at both ends by working a day job and bouncing at night, Carroll set his sights on a more secure and rewarding occupation: the New Jersey State Police.[327]

Carroll's acceptance letter into training arrived in the fall of 1978. When Bill entered the academy as a member of the ninety-fourth class, the dropout rate was 50 percent. The training was grueling, but there was no doubt that Bill Carroll was going to graduate. Trooper William Carroll was bestowed badge #3296.[328]

On January 27, 1979, Trooper Carroll reported to Troop B headquarters to receive his first assignment in the Northern Troop. Six months later, on June 30, 1979, Carroll was transferred to Troop C and worked in it for three uninterrupted years.[329]

During this time, Carroll went out one night with a few of his squad members for drinks. There he met a pretty woman named Michelle Andes. Michelle was captivated by his good looks and hazel eyes. They hit it off and exchanged phone numbers. Michelle waited for him to call, but he never called. A few weeks later, the two ran into each other, and he asked for her number once again, claiming that he had lost it.[330]

Bill Carroll arrived on his first date with Michelle carrying a single yellow rose. "I want you to be my friend first," he told her. It was smooth, and "it worked," said Michelle. The two dated for four years and became engaged on Christmas 1982. During their courtship, the two spent

Bill Carroll. *Courtesy of Christopher Carroll.*

hours upon hours together, despite Carroll's agonizing rotating shifts. Michelle worked as a nurse, a steady 11:00 p.m. to 7:00 a.m. shift, which compounded matters.[331]

On October 29, 1982, Personnel Order No. 255 noted the initial words in what was to be the last chapter in Bill Carroll's life—Carroll was being transferred to the New Jersey Turnpike, Troop D.[332]

Carroll's first months on the major thoroughfare were met with typical New Jersey weather conditions and a flood of accidents and motorist aid assists. History records many troopers losing their lives here on this long stretch of macadam. In May 1984, Trooper Carlos Negron #3656 was gunned down and added to that list. For Carroll, it was a dangerous but rewarding assignment.[333]

On Saturday, May 26, 1984, he and Michelle were wed in a ceremony at Saint Peter's Church in New Brunswick. Family and friends gathered at the reception in the Marriott in Somerset, with 250 people in attendance. Afterward, it was off to Disney World for a week and then on to the Bahamas

Tracking escaped prisoners, Farrington Lake, New Brunswick. *Courtesy of Christopher Carroll.*

at Paradise Island for another. Always attentive to details, it was Bill and not Michelle who made all the arrangements.[334]

Michelle and Bill had a long courtship, filled with love and an eagerness to begin their life together. It took five years for them to finally wed, and then they began looking forward to building a family together. Michelle looked back on her relationship with Carroll. "Billy was big, bulky and could fill a doorway," she said laughing. "He would scare the crap out of a lot of people...But with his sandy brown hair and hazel eyes," he was really a soft, gentle man with a "big heart." Michelle was once told by a trooper that in the academy Bill would "box the crap out of you," and then you would see him praying with his rosaries at night. "I still have those rosaries," said Michelle. The softer side of Bill Carroll showed a man who loved animals. "Every time I came back to our apartment, I would find a dog...'I found the dog,' he would say." Thinking back on those times, Michelle laughed. "How many dogs can a person find?"

One morning, while she was getting ready for work, she found a snapping turtle in the shower. The brawly trooper had found it on the road and wanted to save it. "He was a really sweet man," but he "wouldn't let a lot of people know that, but he was." Seven weeks after their joyful wedding, the day of July 12, 1984, arrived.[335]

Trooper Bill Carroll was in good spirits and looking forward to working his shift. As he prepared troop car 822 for his tour, the weather was nice, with a clear blue sky. The first portion of his shift was uneventful, and then, at about 9:23 a.m., Carroll stopped a Kenilworth tractor-trailer for a motor vehicle violation. The vehicle pulled over at milepost 76.1 on the northbound portion of the turnpike, with the trooper pulling his car in front of the truck.[336]

After speaking with the driver about the violation, Carroll started to walk back to his vehicle. As he did, a truck drifted onto the shoulder and struck Carroll, throwing the giant of a man like a rag doll.[337]

Rushed to the hospital alive and conscious, Bill was complaining of pain in both legs and his left arm. A lesser man wouldn't have made it to the hospital; the injuries he sustained were fatal. Doctors fought drastically to save the young man via a long operation to mend his many injuries. As a testament to his strength, Carroll survived the operation. However, doctors couldn't stabilize him. Troopers from around the state arrived to donate blood for no less than forty blood transfusions that were administered. In the end, it was too much for even Bill Carroll to overcome.[338]

Trooper William Lawrence Carroll Jr. #3296 was laid to rest in a grave that his father helped to dig at Saint Peter's Cemetery.[339]

Days later, Michelle opened her mailbox and received her wedding pictures from the photographer. She and Bill had been waiting for them to arrive so that they could include them with the thank-you cards. Michelle was beside herself; after thinking a bit, she knew what to do. "I sent out the wedding thank-you cards because that was happy…and then I sent out the funeral cards."

RAID

Albert J. Mallen Sr. #2753

Few Jersey trooper detectives have been killed in the line of duty. Albert John Mallen was one of these brave men. Born on January 16, 1949, his father, John Joseph, was of Irish and English descent and worked as a bread man selling Freihofer and Bond Bread. His mother, Irene Rose (née Aubertin), was of French Canadian heritage and was a housewife. Seven children were born to Albert and Irene: Janet, Joan, Albert, Jackie, Jane, Janice and Joyce. The couple lived in a white three-story home with a finished basement equipped with a bar and a pool table at 20 West Decatur Avenue, in Pleasantville, New Jersey. Their home was located in a quiet community founded on an old stagecoach route. The Mallen home was next door to the Saint Peter's Catholic Church.[340]

The patriarch of the family worked mainly at night, delivering his bread. Irene made sure that the children did not disturb Dad while he was sleeping. The home was filled with an Old World atmosphere—rather, children were seen and not heard.[341]

The entire Mallen crew attended Saint Peter's Catholic School across the street from their home. There, Albert served as an altar boy. As a child, his hair was blond, and he was an average adolescent. The parochial education that Mallen received at Saint Peter's forged his character and helped give the man a moral clarity that would sustain him throughout his lifetime. In essence, his education and religious upbringing became his guiding light.[342]

Getting into his black-and-white. *Courtesy of Peggy Mallen.*

Living next door to the Mallens were eight cousins. Needless to say, West Decatur Avenue was a busy street, with kids running about. Living close to his aunt and uncle and cousins made for a wonderful environment, with adjourning backyards. In the yard sat a cement pond in which the kids swam, and they played ball in Saint Peter's parking lot.[343]

After Saint Peter's, Albert attended the Holy Spirit High School in town. He enjoyed many sports activities, except for football—his mother was afraid that he would get injured. There Mallen grew not only physically but intellectually as well. He prospered in his social abilities, and his Catholicism provided him a strong moral character. Al Mallen was the type of person who didn't follow a crowd. He paved his own path, strong in his convictions—he was a leader, not a follower. During his tenure at Holy Spirit, Mallen was bestowed the honor of receiving the school's Monsignor Henry Award for having demonstrated strong religious convictions. In his final year, his mother allowed him to play football, and he enjoyed the rigors of that sport.[344]

The photo next to Mallen's senior picture in his 1967 yearbook is of Margaret Maguire. The two obviously knew each other but did not date. Margaret (or Peggy, as she is called) admitted that she had a crush on Albert all throughout senior year. Interestingly, Al Mallen did not date his entire four years of high school, and it is believed by some that he was contemplating priesthood. Peggy hoped that she would be asked by him to the senior prom, but Mallen did not attend the event.[345]

It is around this point in time that John and Irene were told that their precious daughter Joan had Hodgkin's disease—a fight she lost, passing away at the age of nineteen. Unimaginable grief and heartache consumed the Mallen family—at times the pain tested their faith. However, in the end, it was faith that brought them through.[346]

In June 1967, with her graduation, Peggy Maguire gave up all hope of dating Al Mallen. When Mallen graduated, he stood six feet tall, weighed 220 pounds and had light-brown hair, green eyes and a muscular physique. He was a handsome man, and Peggy knew that he wouldn't last long on the open market. So, when her phone rang in August, and it was him on the other end asking her on a date, she was ecstatic. From that moment, the two were a mainstay.[347]

The United States was embroiled in the Vietnam conflict for most of Mallen's school years. The times were troubling, as they have so often been throughout American history. History has proven time and again that patriots come forth to defend the homeland and the interests of the United States. So, in the fall of 1968, Albert Mallen enlisted in the United States Marine Corps. During his training at Parris Island, Peggy's phone once again rang; it was Al, proposing.[348]

The two were wed on a windy but bright and sunny Saturday afternoon on March 29, 1969, at Our Lady Star of the Sea Church in Atlantic City. Mallen stood in full military garb with his best friend, Jim Gross, beside him. Gross had been wounded in Vietnam and stood with his arm in a sling—a reminder of the danger that Mallen was about to face. Father Overton J. Jones, who had been a high school teacher of Al's, performed the service. A reception was held at the Margate Mariner, overlooking the Margate Bay. The two went to historic Boston for their honeymoon.[349]

Mallen was sent to Vietnam as a member of the Third Marine Division—interestingly, the same division in which Philip Lamonaco #2663 was serving. While he was overseas, Peggy gave birth to a daughter, Jennifer Joan Mallen, in December 1969. After completing his tour in Vietnam, Mallen was transferred to Okinawa, Japan.[350]

Upon his discharge, Sergeant Mallen had earned the National Defense Service Medal, the RVN Cross of Gallantry (with palm and frame), the Rifle Sharpshooters Badge, the Vietnam Service Medal (with a cluster) and the Combat Action Ribbon, which signified his part in ground combat.[351]

Back in the States, he resumed his normal hobbies and interests, ranging from sports to going out and listening to live bands at the Melody Lounge in Atlantic City. Al Mallen never had a lot of friends, but the ones he chose were loyal and lifelong. "Albert was very strong in his opinions and always let you know how he felt. In high school, he did not follow the crowd [and] he let his conscience be his guide." Al was "honest and loyal" and "hated cheap people."[352]

While working as a stock clerk at a supermarket, Mallen filled out an application to the state police. He and Peggy had moved around the corner from her parents and were living in Peggy's grandmother's basement apartment on Chelsea Avenue in Atlantic City. Al loved sunbathing at the Chelsea Avenue Beach. He had grown close to his in-laws, Edward and Margie, and they loved him like a son. It was a nice family environment for Peggy and Al, living so close to her family.[353]

Mallen was accepted as a member of the eighty-fifth state police class and was trained at the new Sea Girt Academy, which opened in July 1970. He graduated on Saturday, June 26, 1971, and was given badge #2753. A week later, their second child, Albert Jr., was born.[354]

Mallen's first day on the job was on Monday, June 28, 1971, and he was assigned to the Port Norris Station in Cumberland County. Here the twenty-two-year-old trooper began what would become an impressive career. January 1972 saw Mallen transferred to the Cape May Court House, where he worked for two years before being sent to Tuckerton in January 1974. Mallen would wrap up his uniform duty working five years out on the Atlantic City Expressway.[355]

While working his job as a trooper, Mallen found time to attend Stockton State College in Galloway, New Jersey, seeking an undergraduate degree in criminal justice. It is important to note that few in the organization had a college degree. The outfit didn't have educational requirements, which led many to gain employment right out of high school. In June 1976,

Mallen graduated Stockton, and the following fall, his third child, Michael John Mallen, was born. Michael was born with a major heart defect and only one kidney and had to be rushed to the Saint Christopher's Hospital for Children in Philadelphia. Doctors at first didn't think that the child would survive; and one can only imagine the emotions and worry that befell Peggy and Al. To get them through this troubling time, they relied on their faith.[356]

In November 1976, Mallen enlisted in the New Jersey Army National Guard, where he once again stepped foot onto the training facility at Sea Girt, which is shared by the Guard. Al began as a sergeant with the 253rd Transportation Company out of the Cape May Court House. This position would bring extra income into their household for their family.[357]

Military portrait. *Courtesy of Peggy Mallen.*

By early 1977, Sergeant Mallen's exceptional leadership was noticed by the guard, and he was encouraged to attend Officers Candidate School. In February 1978, he and Peggy purchased a four-bedroom ranch with one bath and an eat-in kitchen in Egg Harbor Township. It was a perfect starter home and served their needs well. The Mallen children were sent to the Saint Joseph's Grammar School in Somers Point, and Grandma Irene Mallen remained close by to babysit.[358]

On June 4, 1978, Albert Mallen was commissioned a second lieutenant in a ceremony at the Sea Girt facility. Peggy was working in the Golden Nugget Hotel Casino in Atlantic City to bring in extra income. By the middle of 1980, the state police assigned Al Mallen to its Criminal Investigations Section, where he worked in the Narcotics Bureau. As a "Narco" detective, Mallen worked a series of undercover operations, as well as investigations centering on the narcotics trade. From late 1983 to early 1984, Mallen worked to expose a dirty medical doctor and a registered pharmacist who together carried out an elaborate drug distribution network. This successful investigation saw the arrest and conviction of both the doctor and the pharmacist and shut down the entire network. Another assignment, dubbed "Operation Mole," had Mallen focusing on subjects with ties to the Genovese organized crime family. Through this intense and exhaustive case, Mallen uncovered crimes including murder, extortion, robbery and narcotics. When the case wrapped up, eighteen people had been arrested. Yet another investigation lasted four months, with Mallen and his team arresting ten associates and members of the Gambino organized crime family.[359]

The success Mallen had in the outfit was paralleled in the National Guard with his rise to captain. At home, the concern for Michael's health weighed heavily on his and Peggy's mind. With the passing of time, Michael's condition improved. However, a long-term survival guarantee could not be given by the doctors. Despite the pressure, their household was always filled with good spirits and cheer.[360]

Holidays were always special, and Halloween brought all of the family to the Mallen household; nieces and nephews trick-or-treated, and afterward Peggy and Al would order pizza and soda. Needless to say, Christmas was even more festive.[361]

A father and his children. *Courtesy of Peggy Mallen.*

Throughout 1984, Mallen worked steadily on various drug investigations, and by August 1985, he and his unit were working on a large-scale case that involved an illicit drug manufacturing ring with ties to organized crime. The legwork in the case led Mallen and other state police detectives to an apartment in Westville, New Jersey, where they suspected a methamphetamine laboratory was operating. The detectives had done their homework and knew that the suspects involved were Thomas Baldinio and Dominic Schiavo, both in their early fifties and with criminal records. Clint Pagano said it best: "When you deal with degenerates, and that's what drug dealers are, you have to anticipate violence, and sometimes it's impossible to ward it off."[362]

It was Wednesday, August 28, 1985, when Mallen and his band of troopers decided to execute a search warrant on 225 Station Avenue in Westville. Detective Mallen and Detective Sergeant Gerald Lauther entered the upstairs hallway, where they spotted Thomas Baldinio exiting his apartment. The two lawmen grabbed Baldinio and threw him up against the wall. Then, out of the shadows, Dominic Schiavo charged the two with a shotgun chambering it as he moved toward them. The two detectives positioned themselves behind the doorway, with Mallen standing and Lauther taking a knee. Schiavo blasted a single shot before being shot by a hail of bullets. When the smoke cleared, Al Mallen had been fatally shot in the head.[363]

Investigators later discovered that Schiavo (who survived his wounds) was a longtime associate of Raymond ("Long John") Martorano, a lieutenant in the Philadelphia-based Bruno crime family. An additional raid on Schiavo's apartment in Washington Township revealed an active methamphetamine laboratory.[364]

Later that day, Peggy Mallen returned from picking up birthday favors for Michael's upcoming party and was met by her mother-in-law and Mallen's sergeant, Kenny Prescott #1983. Her world had changed forever.[365]

Albert John Mallen Sr. was laid to rest at Holy Cross Cemetery on U.S. 40 in Hamilton Township in Atlantic County, New Jersey. He was thirty-six years old. The Bellmawr Station was dedicated to the memory of Al Mallen. At that service, Peggy Mallen said: "It is important that we let the world know that our adversary has not won. We must let them know that we have become stronger. I say to you, the members of the New Jersey State Police, pick up Albert's shield and carry on for him to the best of your ability."[366]

EVEN THE SIMPLEST CALL CAN BE PERILOUS

THEODORE J. MOOS #2706

In February 1987, Teddy Moos was running a squad of six troopers at Bellmawr Station. With sixteen years experience under his belt, he was eagerly waiting to be promoted to sergeant. Moos had been off patrol for a period and had been working in the Educational Services Unit (ESU); however, he returned to uniform patrol for his sergeants stripes. A natural leader with an easy deportment, Moos was well liked and admired within the organization. He always had a good sense of humor and a strong devotion to community. Those who knew him knew that he was sincere.[367]

Theodore Joseph Moos was born on Saturday, September 4, 1943, in Stratford, New Jersey. His father, George, emigrated from Germany to America with his parents as a teenager. George Moos married Catherine (née Hatch), a woman of Irish descent. The couple lived in Clementon in Camden County, New Jersey. George owned a hardware and feed store in town that supported him and Catherine and their children: Ellen, Joseph and Theodore. The family lived in a comfortable home at 127 Ohio Avenue. George had been previously married and had a daughter, Irene, who lived with them as well. Irene, who was about fifteen years older than Teddy, took on the big sister role to her little siblings.[368]

The Moos children attended the Gibbs Public Grammar School. In high school, Teddy became a starter quarterback on the freshmen team, whereas his older brother, Joseph, was a junior and played halfback on varsity. While playing sports, Moos met a majorette who caught his eye.[369]

Teddy, Nancy and the children. *Courtesy of Nancy Moos.*

Nancy Walton was always on the sidelines when Teddy Moos was out on the field. The two became friends and nothing more at first. Teddy also played basketball, ran track and wrestled while in school. All the while, Nancy continued her role as a majorette on the sidelines. She remembers Moos as being very athletic and a fast sprinter in track. Moos's sports activities were marked by his mounting trophy collection. Sitting in a sophomore English class, the stars aligned for Teddy and Nancy.[370]

The teacher put together a play called *Life with Father* and cast Nancy and Teddy as husband and wife. "That's when I really got to know him," Nancy said. Their roles in the play foreshadowed the future.[371]

During his sophomore year, Teddy and his brother, Joseph, played varsity football together, with Joseph being named all-American player. George and Catherine enjoyed seeing their two sons play together. By sophomore year, Teddy Moos stood six feet tall and weighed 180 pounds. He had brown hair, blue eyes and a fair complexion—a good catch, and Nancy knew it. Their courtship epitomized the "high school sweetheart romance."[372]

In his senior year on the football team, Moos became captain and continued performing with impressive play as the quarterback. One game in particular, Nancy said, she will never forget. It was Thanksgiving 1960, and his team was behind by one score, with Moos moving his team slowly down the field. Within seconds of the game ending Teddy ran the football in for a winning touchdown. The crowd went wild. When the game ended, "He picked me up and swung me around. It was like a movie," said Nancy. In June 1961, both Nancy and Teddy graduated Overbrook High.[373]

During the summer, Moos's parents moved their family to Florida; without a job or a place to stay, Moos moved with them. This put a temporary rift between him and Nancy. Then, surprisingly, Moos moved out to Indiana, where his brother had been living. The two had always been close. Working out in Indiana for a period of time made Teddy realize how much he missed Nancy, and he moved back in December 1961 and stayed with Nancy's grandparent.[374]

The eighteen-year-old began working on an assembly line for the Owens-Corning Fiberglass Company, which is the largest manufacturer of fiberglass and is known for its "pink" installation. At night, Moos attended the Camden County Community College. The divide between him and Nancy had mended, and they were married on Saturday, August 25, 1962, at the Laurel Springs Presbyterian Church. A reception followed at the Silver Lake Inn in Clementon, with a honeymoon in the Poconos.[375]

The couple lived in an apartment complex on Broad Street in Berlin but, after a year and a half, purchased a home at 105 Ridgewood Avenue in Berlin. By this time, Moos was a lab technician at Owens-Corning, and Nancy was pregnant. Teddy Moos began talking to Nancy about the state police and his interest, an interest that can be traced back to high school. "He talked about it right after we got married," said Nancy. "But the money was not real good, and he didn't think we could afford it…so he put it off." After nearly two years together, Stacey Ann Moos was born to the couple in July 1964. The next three years saw the state police being put on the back burner and

Theodore Moos #2706. *Courtesy of Nancy Moos.*

work continuing at Owens-Corning. In October 1967, Shelly Ann was born. By 1968, Moos was growing tired of his job despite the fact that he got promoted. The state police once again became a topic of conversation between him and Nancy.[376]

History records Theodore Moos graduating from the eighty-fourth state police class on Thursday, March 5, 1970. Afterward, a large party saw Nancy and the girls giving Moos an English bulldog (he had always wanted one). The puppy was white, and Nancy put the colors of the "outfit" (blue and gold) on the dog's collar. Trooper Moos #2706 began his first tour at Malaga in Troop A. In August, Moos was sent to Woodstown Station, only to move again the following March to Mays Landing. In August 1972, a son, Theodore Jay, was born.[377]

Throughout the decade, Moos worked a number of assignments, including Malaga, New Brunswick and Hammonton, to name but a few. Meanwhile, at home, time was spent with Nancy and the children. Moos coached his children's sports teams, as well as other teams. Teddy always wanted to help others and enjoyed being a part of his community. The most rewarding thing in his life was watching his children grow. Yearly vacations were taken to Brigantine Beach and Ocean City, both in New Jersey. Beginning in 1974, Teddy and Nancy took their family every year to Disney World.[378]

At home, Moos could often be seen cooking. He enjoyed it and was good at it. At times, he could be a jokester, recalled Nancy: "He would heat up milk and pour it into his cereal, saying he wanted a cooked meal." But most of all, Moos had a laid-back nature. "He was the easiest-going individual," said Nancy. One time, Nancy sold all of the furniture in the living room to someone who had wanted it without telling Teddy. When Moos came home, he asked about it. He was not bothered or annoyed. "He was so good and easygoing…he just went outside and got a lawn chair to sit on." When his dog got sick, he carried the pet to chemotherapy for two years. When his pet died, he built a casket and buried the dog in the backyard.[379]

The year 1986 was a wonderful one for the Moos family, filled with celebrations; all three children graduated from each of their respected schools, and their daughter, Shelly, got married, with Teddy walking her down the aisle. The year ended on a sad note, with Nancy's father passing away, but they enjoyed the holiday season together and were looking forward to the upcoming year.[380]

On the evening of January 28, 1987, Moos wasn't feeling well but insisted on going in even when Nancy asked him to stay home. If going

Celebrating his forty-first birthday. *Courtesy of Nancy Moos.*

to work wasn't draining enough, this particular night Moos was working the overnight shift.[381]

Directing traffic at an accident scene is not glorious work nor what many troopers enjoy. Nonetheless, it is a necessity of the job. Records have Trooper Moos doing just that on January 30 at 1:00 a.m. on Highway 42 at milepost 14.1 in Bellmawr Borough on the northbound side of the roadway. There, a drunken driver struck Trooper Moos, causing severe injuries. "He was conscious when I got to the hospital," recalled Nancy. "I got to talk to him…he was shaking his head like he was frustrated and angry this happened." The first day or two after the accident, Moos was awake, and Nancy communicated with him. However, when doctors had to put a breathing tube down his throat, they put him into a paralyzing state where he was aware of what was going on but couldn't move. "I encouraged him…but things kept getting worse and worse." When doctors had to amputate his leg, they "asked me to go in and tell Teddy." She will never forget that moment. She tried to lighten the mood by telling him, "You're still going to clean the damn pool." Moos couldn't talk, but "a tear ran down his face." After nearly a month of doctors trying to save his life, Theodore Moos succumbed to his injuries on Friday, February 27, at the age of forty-three.[382]

DIRECTIONS, PLEASE?

Thomas J. Hanratty #4971

Thomas Joseph Hanratty was a young man who enjoyed quiet events, sports and quality time with his family. He was a trooper who came to the vocation as a matter of happenstance rather than desire. The young man vacillated on what to do with his life. Policing was in his blood—his maternal grandfather was an Elizabeth, New Jersey police officer, as were his uncles. Tommy, as his friends called him, was born in Elizabeth, a busy metropolis. His grandparents, Thomas John and Dorothy (née Killimet), emigrated from Northern Ireland to America. Thomas worked in America as a machinist and died at the early age of forty-nine. His son (Tommy's father), Thomas John Jr., grew to adulthood without the influence of a father and relied on his mother's strong devotion and loving nature. As an adult, Thomas John met Francis Brennan, an attractive brunette, and she captured his heart. Nancy, as Tom called her, had deep roots in the city of Elizabeth. She was of Irish and English descent; her father, Thomas, was an Elizabeth police officer, and her uncle would rise through that same department to police chief.[383]

Thomas John and Nancy courted for a time and wed in a ceremony in Elizabeth. Then they moved into a small apartment in the city. Thomas worked as a local laborer for Union #394 and remained in this vocation his entire life. On Thursday, September 21, 1967, their first child, Thomas Joseph, was born. Two years later, another son, Timothy, arrived and was followed a few years later by yet another boy whom they named Terrence.

Thomas and Nancy pinched their pennies with the hopes of one day buying a home of their own. In 1972, they had to move to a larger apartment on Bailey Street to accommodate their growing family. In 1974, the Hanrattys purchased a home at 826 Bailey Avenue in the city, and here in this spacious three-bedroom colonial, Tommy Hanratty grew to adulthood.[384]

Tommy Hanratty was a social little kid who mingled well with others. He loved playing with other children and thrived in school. Tommy had a world of activities and a large group of friends. Above all, Tommy was close to his two brothers. As an older brother, he looked after Timmy and Terry. Both brothers used their older brother as a sounding board when

The Hanratty brothers. *Courtesy of Nancy Hanratty.*

they had problems. Tommy always offered advice but chose a democratic way to deliver those words of wisdom. In turn, he taught them to be analytical and to work through their problems. To this day, Timmy and Terry credit their older brother with helping them to be critical thinkers.[385]

The years passed, and the young boy enjoyed sports and was a very active participant in most of the organized sports activities—that is, except football, as mom had forbidden it. Bailey Avenue was a nice street where children of all ages played well together, and Tommy could always be seen out there with his friends. He would often teach those younger than him how to play ball and enjoyed being the role model.[386]

Throughout school, Hanratty had above-average grades, and in high school, he entertained thoughts of becoming a schoolteacher. When he was sixteen, Tommy began working as a lifeguard at the YMCA in Union, New Jersey. This would be one of only two jobs that he would hold in his lifetime.[387]

In June 1985, Hanratty graduated and spent the entire summer relaxing, spending time with his family and hanging out with his friends.[388]

At eighteen, Hanratty was an impressive figure, standing nearly six feet tall and weighing 180 pounds, with an athlete's build. He had light-brown hair and blue eyes and was a handsome-looking Irishman. His father instilled in him old-fashioned family values that he displayed well in adulthood. Tommy idolized his father and adored his mother. For the Hanrattys, family was the center of the universe, and this rang true for Tommy as well.[389]

In September 1985, Hanratty began studying teaching at Kean College in Union Township. "He always wanted to be a teacher," said Nancy. At Kean, he could pursue his aspirations. Throughout his three years there, Hanratty focused on becoming a teacher. He supported himself with his lifeguard position at the YMCA. Then, out of the blue, a friend of his told Hanratty about an upcoming trooper test. Tommy said, "Oh well, I'll try it," recalled his mother.[390]

Tommy Hanratty entered the rolls of the New Jersey State Police on a cold winter's day in a graduation ceremony on Friday, February 10, 1989, at Fort Dix, New Jersey, and was given badge #4971. Afterward, a party for just immediate family and close friends was held at the Hanratty house; Tommy preferred small gatherings, as he viewed large parties to be annoyances. Joining him at the party was a young German woman named Crystal Boght, whom Tommy had been dating for nearly a year.[391]

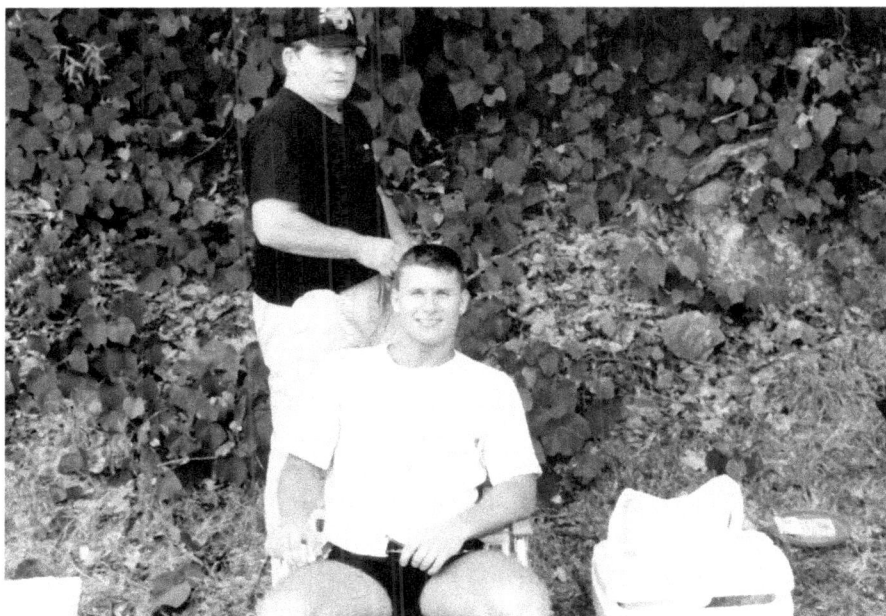

Tommy and his dad. *Courtesy of Nancy Hanratty.*

Hanratty's first position was out of the Washington Station, which was responsible for patrolling a few highways and the many small hamlets that occupy the farmlands and wooded area of Warren County. Tommy was assigned a trooper coach to teach him the tricks of the trade; Trooper James Dobak #4287 looks fondly back on the time he spent training Hanratty. "He learned quickly," said Dobak. Now a seasoned sergeant, Dobak became close friends with Hanratty. Tommy was always personable and eager to help others, recalled Dobak. Often after working the evening shift, the squad of troopers would head out for a bite to eat and have a few drinks, and the senior troopers would tell "war stories."[392]

During his career, Tommy became close friends with Steven Parisi #4328, Fred Womack #4260 and Pete Brown #4275. Tommy's mother, Nancy, remembered Freddie Womack and Tommy spending a lot of time together. The two troopers would double-date and play basketball together. Steve Parisi and Hanratty became partners and developed a friendship. Although the trooper was making new friends, he never abandoned his childhood friends.[393]

Hanratty enjoyed wearing the uniform of a Jersey trooper and looked fit doing so. As a trooper, Hanratty was stern when necessary, lenient when appropriate and compassionate when needed. After the Washington Station, the organization moved Hanratty to the Summerville Station. As Hanratty pulled up to the historic old station in his steel-gray sports Camaro, he had to ponder his future here at Somerville.[394]

The Somerville Station whispers echoes of years gone by; Robert Coyle #238 and "Big" Mike Beylon #318 patrolled their last here. These small corridors remind troopers of the earliest days of the outfit. It was now late 1989, and the organization was represented by troopers like Tommy Hanratty.[395]

By 1991, Tommy and Crystal had broken up, and he soon began dating Mary Fiorito. It was about this time when Nancy said that her son began rethinking his future. "I think he liked it, but he was getting ready to go back to college and finish." Nancy remembered a conversation she had with Tommy. "I think it really wasn't for him," she said of the state police. "I know he used to say, 'Mom, it's very dangerous…but I love the job.'" From a mother's perspective, Nancy said, "When a boy is twenty-one, I think you need a little bit more time…he was young, I think he should have stayed in college longer." Needless to say, Tommy chose to become a trooper—fate beckoned.[396]

April 2, 1992, wasn't a typical April day in the Garden State; a light snow was covering the landscape in white. Hanratty had been assigned

Trooper Hanratty #4971. *Courtesy of Nancy Hanratty.*

Interstate 78 and had been patrolling. At about 4:30 p.m., he stopped a car for a violation.[397]

After doing so, a passing motorist stopped to ask Trooper Hanratty for directions. Always willing to help, Hanratty walked over and provided assistance. After helping the motorist, he began to walk back to his troop car and was struck by another car. The impact caused his death.[398]

An investigation was conducted, and it was discovered that the driver of that vehicle had been drinking and was on medication. The effect of the two—it was suspected—combined to cause the driver to veer off the road and kill the trooper. As a result, the driver was charged with death by auto.[399]

The news of their son's death devastated the Hanrattys—Tommy's father in particular. "It just broke his heart," said Nancy. "He never recovered."[400]

The service for Trooper Hanratty was attended by thousands of people, and as they carried his casket out of the church, the "Battle Hymn of the Republic" was played. More than six hundred cars drove in the procession to Hanratty's final resting place in Colonia at the Gertrude Cemetery, which is in Woodbridge, New Jersey.[401]

Days after the funeral, Nancy Hanratty had a conversation with Trooper Pete Brown #4275. "He said to me, 'Mrs. Hanratty, Thomas was always worried…if anything ever happens to me, make sure they do the right thing, and do a good investigation.'" Needless to say, the investigation was lackluster, followed by an equally poor performance at trial.[402]

On March 16, 1993, after a jury deliberated for fourteen hours over two days, the driver was acquitted of all criminal charges; he was, however, found guilty of having an open container of alcohol in his car and was sentenced to ten days community service at a local cemetery.[403]

In April 1995, Tommy's little brother, Timothy Hanratty #5276, followed in his footsteps and graduated from the 115th class.

"A SMILE THAT COULD LIGHT UP THE WORLD"

MARVIN R. McCLOUD #4718

To quote the *Courier-Post*:

> *Perhaps the most moving tributes from the nearly 1,000 people at Trooper Marvin R. McCloud's funeral…came in the prayerful words of his two daughters—Tiffany, 12 and Candice, 6;*

> *Dear Lord, We thank you for blessing us with Marvin McCloud as our father, he was the best Daddy, Lord…Dad, we salute and thank you for taking us to the movies, skating, helping us with our homework, and all those swimming lessons.* [404]

Marvin McCloud was an "upbeat man" who reportedly had a "smile that could light up the world." Born on Thursday, June 4, 1964, in Camden, New Jersey, his parents, Edward and Marva, had three children: Marvin, Carla and Latira. Marvin was raised in the urban community of Camden and loved it there. As a child, he attended the public grammar school and then went to the Camden County Vocational and Technical High School in nearby Pennsauken. Growing up in the city wasn't easy for the young kid, with all the temptations of gangs and drug use, but Marvin McCloud stayed above these evils. Instead, he built himself up both mentally and physically. [405]

When Marvin was old enough to make a difference, he volunteered to become a "Big Brother" in the Big Brothers Big Sisters program in

Trooper Marvin R. McCloud #4718. *Courtesy of the New Jersey State Police.*

Camden. Marvin had a desire to help others, and he had instilled within himself a sense of community. McCloud knew how tough it could be growing up in the city and wanted to set a standard for others to follow. As the years passed, Marvin became an avid weightlifter and enjoyed a steady workout routine.[406]

By the age of eighteen, Marvin had been dating a young teenager named Crystal Waters, and in July 1982, the couple had their first child together, daughter Tiffany. After graduating from high school, McCloud got a job assembling electronics while at the same time attending Seton Hall University. Marvin worked six years in the electronics field and was enjoying watching his little daughter grow.[407]

> *We thank you* [God], *because he was a kind, firm yet gentle dad. Our dad was someone we could always depend on for everything. He always* [encouraged] *and supported us in everything we did.*[408]

In the years that had passed since the birth of Tiffany, Marvin had marveled at what was to come. Most amusing to him was watching his little girl grow. Within the man was willingness to help others, a sense of community. One of his sayings was, "You have to believe in humanity, or there will be no humanity left." In this vein, McCloud applied to the state police so he could greater serve his community.

On July 19, 1987, members of the 109th class began training in Sea Girt, New Jersey. The training lasted four grueling months, cumulating in a graduation ceremony that took place on Thursday, November 19, 1987. Marvin Robert McCloud #4718 was now part of the elite organization.[409]

144

Saturday, November 21, saw McCloud put on his uniform for the first day of patrol out of the Tuckerton Station. There McCloud went through the "Trooper Coach Program" and successfully completed his final phase of trooper training. In June, the state police transferred him to the Bridgeton Station. Come July 1988, Marvin became a father once again with the birth of Candice. With a secure job and a steady paycheck, Marvin and Crystal married on Thursday, August 4, 1988. Marvin used to refer to Tiffany and Candice as his "little girls." He wouldn't let them out of his sight; they were light that fueled his world.[410]

> We had a lot of fun with you, Daddy. We thank you for the karate lessons and our special trip to Disney World last year.[411]

As Tiffany and Candice grew, the doting dad could be seen helping them with homework, playing games and enjoying time with them. He was a proud dad who tried to instill in his girls the understanding of right and wrong.[412]

> And, Dad we especially thank you for loving us so much, you spent a lot of time talking to us about growing up to be "good girls."

In February 1989, McCloud was sent to the Bellmawr Station, where he would spend the majority of his tenure with the organization. Besides his commitment to his family and the state police, Marvin had hobbies about which he was passionate. As mentioned, he enjoyed weightlifting, but a more peaceful pastime for him was playing chess; it was a game that challenged him mentally, and he used to love playing with others. A sensitive side also existed in the strong man in blue. He liked to write poetry and had hoped one day to have one of his poems published. Jazz music was also a favorite. While at Bellmawr, McCloud developed strong relationships with many troopers that remained with him once his time there had concluded. In February 1994, McCloud was transferred to the Moorestown Station in Troop D.[413]

The Moorestown Station proved to be a busy assignment for McCloud, but he enjoyed working there. In addition to his duties as a trooper and father, McCloud found time to work as a fitness instructor for a Camden City YMCA. He had an amazing commitment toward helping others, and this was an extension of that ambition. His family said that Marvin "was our Rock of Gibraltar, who would give the shirt off his back." His colleagues said that he "was the kind of guy that would do anything for you." And his commitment to his community was highlighted in the remarks of Reverend Jones, who said, "Marvin would have me tell all of you that this was his city…[and] that there is some good in Camden."[414]

On Sunday, June 4, 1995, Marvin McCloud celebrated his thirty-first birthday. He had come a long way in his life and was proud of his children and his accomplishments. The following day, Marvin was back at work and, just before 9:00 a.m., decided to run radar for speeders. In the turnaround at milepost 4.7, he pulled off to do just that. Not long afterward, a Nissan Pathfinder driven by David Whigham of Bellville, New Jersey, left the travel portion of the road and crashed into the rear of McCloud's troop car. The impact was so severe that McCloud died from his injuries one day later.[415]

There wasn't a dry eye in the church when the words of Marvin's little girls were broadcast to the hundreds standing in formation at his funeral:

> *Daddy, we promise to try our best to be "good girls" so that you will always be happy and proud of us…Again, we thank you Lord for our Daddy. And, Dad…we will miss you so much. And we love you Daddy.*[416]

HIGH-SPEED PURSUIT

Francis J. Bellaran #4429

Red Bank, New Jersey, is an affluent suburb in Monmouth County, New Jersey. Records on Red Bank go as far back as the late 1600s, when the town was once part of Shrewsbury Township, which was one of the three original townships in the state. For years, only two buildings stood in Red Bank, and interestingly, one of them was a tavern that sat on the bank of the Navesink River. It is this river that transformed Red Bank from an obscure venue to a bustling town. Throughout the years, droves of boats came to the shores of Red Bank—first sailboats, then steamboats and finally motorboats. Red Bank became known for its textiles, fur and tanning manufacturing, and local fishermen and farmers shipped their products from town over to Manhattan in New York. By the middle of the nineteenth century, the community was experiencing tremendous growth, but near the close of the century, the Raritan and Delaware Bay Railroad came to town and pushed the commercial boating industry out of business. Commercial boating turned into recreational boating, and the Red Bank shores took on a different look. In winter months, ice boating became popular, and in the summer, speedboats came to town, bringing spectators from all around Red Bank to watch the racing.[417]

In the twentieth century, the township was incorporated and was formally christened Red Bank. In December 1923, Red Bank became forever enmeshed with the New Jersey State Police when a young trooper named William Marshall #63 crashed his motorcycle in town and became the first

Daddy's little girl. *Courtesy of the Bellaran family.*

Jersey trooper to die in the line of duty. However, the intertwining between this community and the state police doesn't end here. Forty years later, on July 13, 1963, a small child named Francis J. Bellaran was born in town. Like Marshall before, Bellaran would give his life while wearing the uniform of the Jersey trooper.[418]

Trooper Francis Bellaran's story begins on January 28, 1960, when Francis Anthony Bellaran wed Carol (née Henry). Frank was an ironworker by trade and was once a merchant marine, like his father before him. The surname "Bellaran" has roots from the Philippines.[419]

Frank and Carol had three children together, beginning with Deborah and followed by Francis and Carol Ann. The Bellarans lived in a small home on Morganville Road in Old Bridge, New Jersey. According to Carol Bellaran, her son, Frank, was a handful from the get-go. Family and friends used to call him "Bud," and when he was a toddler, he wandered out of bed and down the road to his grandmother's. "If I took my eyes off of him, he was gone," said Carol. A few years later, the Bellarans bought a large eighteen-acre farm on Kirshman Lane, complete with a variety of farm animals. "We had chickens, horses, cows, pigs and ducks." Animals, Carol recalled, didn't appeal to her son. "Bud didn't want nothing to do with that…Bud was the type of kid who would take a bath and come out dirty."[420]

Bud's role on the farm was to clean out the stalls, cut the grass and rake up. He hated doing his chores, as do most kids growing up. One of the things he enjoyed was hunting with his father; oftentimes they would hunt raccoon. Other hobbies enjoyed by Bud were fishing and skateboarding. He loved to skateboard and even had a large rink set up to accommodate his hobby. "One day," said Carol, "I got a phone call. Frank had broken his teeth from skateboarding." Bud always kept his parents on the edge of their seats. They never knew what he was going to get into. Frank's maternal grandfather, James Patrick Henry, was very close to Bud and bought him a motorcycle. From then on, hours were spent by the young teenager riding through his farmland.[421]

Interestingly, the kid who didn't like animals brought home a stray dog he named Barney, and the two became inseparable. The family had a small motorboat and boated in a nearby creek. There they would go swimming and fishing, and Barney always tagged along, swimming with Bud in the water. These boating trips were joyful events and are today fond memories of the days that have passed.[422]

The Bellaran children came up through the local school system, with Frank proceeding to the Cedar Ridge High School in town. During his senior year, Bud took a photography class in which he met a pretty girl named Judy Volkert. Judy was two years his junior, and their relationship developed over time. They remained acquaintances at first, and it wasn't until after he graduated that he asked Judy on a date.[423]

Right after graduating, Frank followed in his dad's footsteps and began working as an ironworker. Frank obtained his union book out of Saint Johns in Newfoundland, Canada, but worked in and around the tri-state area. Making good money as an ironworker allowed Frank to take Judy out on quality dates. The two went on numerous trips together; from the shores of Lake Hoptacong in New Jersey to the Jersey Shore, they enjoyed their time together. In the winter, the couple headed to Hunter Mountain in New York to ski.[424]

Frank was doing well for himself and decided to live on his own in a condominium at 1215 Wellington Place in Aberdeen, New Jersey. The years quickly passed by, and Frank and Judy were almost always together; there was the occasional breakup every now and then, but their attraction toward each other always brought them back into each other's arms. Their activities continued and soon broadened to farther trips, from exotic vacation spots to road trips. Two of their favorite adventures were in Key West and Myrtle Beach.[425]

Frank was growing tired of his job, partially because he would hear his cousins Vinnie and Ray Bellaran talking about their jobs as troopers. The cousins always looked sharp in their French blue uniforms, and Frank would look on with envy. Before long, he wanted to become part of the state police.[426]

In 1986, Frank Bellaran set out to fulfill that goal, taking and passing the state police examination. He began training as a member of the 106th class and graduated on January 15, 1987. Trooper Bellaran #4429 had taken off his construction helmet and replaced it with a trooper's hat.[427]

Frank's parents had adopted a young boy named Michael, to whom Frank became very close—he enjoyed being the big brother. All the Bellaran children were close and shared in that special bond that only a sibling could understand.[428]

After working a series of stations in Troop C, Bellaran was transferred to Troop E (the Garden State Parkway). Trooper Bellaran's assignment was the Holmdel Station, which is rich in state police history; there John Anderson #1191 worked his last shift. Holmdel Station sat on the ground of the Garden State Arts Center (Now PNC Arts Center). In November 2010, the station was demolished to make way for a New Jersey Turnpike

Vehicle Garage. Sitting just a few feet away from this garage is a state-of-the-art state police facility dedicated to the memory of Francis Bellaran and John Anderson.[429]

The last years of Frank Bellaran's life were spent patrolling out of Holmdel. It was an assignment that he loved. The years passed, and Frank witnessed his share of gory accident scenes and criminal arrests. Being a Jersey trooper does not come without its share of dangers and risks, all of which Frank Bellaran knew. Judy knew this, too, and so did his parents. Regardless of the dangers, troopers take an oath, and many stand fast to their words. Francis Bellaran was one such individual.[430]

Judy and Frank's relationship was partly sewn together from the cloth of the state police. Every year, Troop E holds a holiday party for its personnel, and at one of these events, Frank asked Judy to marry him. Judy remembered this night as if it had happened yesterday: "We were at the state police Christmas party and had eaten dinner when Frank went up to the deejay and called me up. I was sitting in a chair (out in the middle of the dance floor), and right in front of all the troopers, he asked me to marry him." More than one hundred people were there, but

Happy parents. *Courtesy of the Bellaran family.*

151

it was an intimate moment between the two of them. "It felt like it was just he and I," said Judy.[431]

In a ceremony at Saint Clement's Roman Catholic Church in Matawan, the couple exchanged vows. The date was Saturday, May 25, 1991, and a reception followed, capped off by a ten-day honeymoon to the exotic locale of Hawaii. There Judy and Frank went to the island of Maui and rented a jeep, touring the island and making stops along the way at different locations to explore the terrain. They went mountain climbing to see the top of a large waterfall. Another day saw Judy relaxing at the pool, while Frank played golf, a sport he came to love. It was a wonderful honeymoon, and the couple hoped to return one day.[432]

The newlyweds moved into Frank's apartment in Aberdeen for a year and a half before moving to Manasquan, New Jersey, in December 1992. This was Frank's parents' home, but sadly they had broken up. Ultimately, Frank and Judy purchased the house. It was a dream house for both of them. Built in 1854, the home was picturesque and painted gray with white trim and had working burgundy shutters and a large front porch with two deacon's benches. Inside is a large stairway that greets visitors. As homeowners, Judy played the perfect wife and Frank the handyman husband. Bellaran loved working on various projects inside or out. Hours were spent by the off-duty trooper in his yard, cutting grass or planting flowers. "Everything around here was always perfect," said Judy. "He would fit in as much during the day as he could."[433]

The love that Frank and Judy had for each other was realized in June 1993 with the birth of their daughter, Shelby. As Shelby grew, she became attached to her father and he to her. He was a doting dad who couldn't spend enough time with his daughter. She was always by his side. While cutting grass, Shelby rode alongside her dad on the riding mower. The two had a wonderful time together doing "chores." He would even take his little girl to the hardware store with him. Shelby loved putting on her father's state police shoes and hat and walking around. It was an adorable sight, this cute little girl donning her father's state police gear in her diaper. "She was very special to him," said Judy. In March 1996, Judy gave birth to their son, Jared, and Frank was thrilled. He had a boy and a girl. His family was complete. His love for Judy and his children were all he could ever ask for.[434]

The cold winter weather faded into the warmer temperatures of spring, and his little boy was growing quickly. Shelby was growing accustomed to the additional family member, and Frank and Judy were enjoying their parenthood. Seven weeks had passed since Jared's birth, and the couple looked forward to the warmer weather. Maybe they would go on a summer vacation this year; they would certainly spend time enjoying their backyard once the weather warmed.[435]

The events of Monday, May 20, 1997, forever changed the lives of Judy Bellaran and her children. It was an unseasonably warm day, with temperatures lingering in the nineties. Warm days like this would see Frank outside with his daughter. However, he had to work this particular day and was on patrol in his marked troop car on the Garden State Parkway in the Ocean and Monmouth County areas on the parkway.[436]

At about 10:50 a.m., troopers patrolling the area heard Frank's voice come over their state police radio, with the siren sounding in the background. He was in high-speed pursuit of a motorcycle going northbound on the parkway. Frank gave out the plate number, NJ-D5465, which came back as stolen. Chasing the motorcycle at speeds of more than 110 miles per hour, Trooper Bellaran gave periodic updates of his location in a calm and collected voice. Listening to the tape, one wouldn't think that Bellaran was under intense stress. Whatever fear or anxiety Bellaran felt was suppressed by his professionalism.[437]

The last transmission Trooper Bellaran gave was that he was "passing milepost 96.6." Too often, motorists are inattentive and pay little attention to their rear-view mirrors. In fact, if rear-view mirrors were optional, few would have them. As Bellaran chased the speeding cyclist, a motorist pulled directly into his lane of travel, leaving the trooper with the choice of either hitting the car or swerving to avoid impact. Frank Bellaran lost control of his troop car, ran off the road and struck a tree—the impact was so severe that the troop car became wrapped around the tree like a horseshoe. Good Samaritans stopped and pulled the trooper's body out of the vehicle and onto the cool green grass. First aid arrived and transported the injured trooper to the Jersey Shore Medical Center in Neptune, New Jersey.[438]

For three days, doctors worked tirelessly to save Bellaran's life, with more than one hundred people responding to donate blood for Frank, who needed more than sixty pints of blood and forty-seven pints of blood platelets and plasma. In the end, it was too much for his body to handle, and Francis "Bud" Bellaran passed away at the early age of thirty-three.[439]

On Tuesday, May 28, the funeral service was held for Bellaran, and in a tearful service, Reverend Dominick Dellaporte spoke of Bellaran and quoted scripture: "'The greatest gift is to lay down one's life for one's friend.' Frank went out and laid down his life…[he] was a perfectionist…he was meticulous. His career was exemplary. His love and passion for his family and for his job makes Frankie a perfect example for your children, for everyone."

A proud dad. *Courtesy of the Bellaran family.*

Trooper Francis J. Bellaran was buried at Saint Catharine's Cemetery on West Chicago Boulevard in Wall Township, New Jersey.[440]

Nearly a year and a half later, on October 18, 1997, Louis D. Goodman, the operator of the motorcycle that Trooper Bellaran had been chasing, was sentenced to eight years in prison for his role in Bellaran's death. At sentencing, Goodman apologized "for causing the death of State Trooper Francis J. Bellaran…When I come into this courtroom," he said, "I cannot bear to look at the faces of the people around me."[441]

TRAPPED

SCOTT M. GONZALEZ #5059

Scott Gonzalez had it difficult growing up. His father, Valentine, abandoned the family when Scott was thirteen years old, and his mother, Diana, had many jobs to support her family. Valentine and Diana had five children: Valentine, Kenneth, Mark, Susan and Scott. Mark died of an apparent suicide as a teenager.[442]

Scott was born on March 29, 1962, in Passaic, New Jersey, and a year later, history has the Gonzalez family living in Baskin Ridge, which is a subsection of Bernards Township in Somerset County. Diana rode a bicycle every day to get to work. Little Scott attended the public school system and often struggled with his grades. Scott was also on the fence about whether he wanted to befriend the good crowd or bad.[443]

When Valentine left his family, the man severed all ties with his children and even his own mother, who had worked her entire life, at times dyeing her hair so that employers couldn't tell how old she was. Time moved on, and Scott's grandmother had to be placed in a nursing home. However, her grandchildren visited her often. Scott had learned how to cook from her.[444]

In high school, Gonzalez grew from a careless adolescent to a pragmatic adult. Scott would defend the weaker and less fortunate when they were picked on by bullies. Rather than cast a blind eye to the bullying behavior, Scott would intervene. "There was a girl in school who was sickly and often teased. Scott befriended her and would protect her from tauntings." In

Sketch from a photo. *Courtesy of Maureen Gonzalez.*

junior year, Scott decided to concentrate more on his grades and turned his academic standing around.[445]

In June 1980, Scott Gonzalez graduated from high school and began working in the construction trade. Throughout the next decade, Scott had taken the written examination for trooper several times but fell short on each attempt. As luck would have it, Scott finally passed the test for the 113th class; however, because of financial problems, the class was put on hold. Four years would pass before members of that class received their invitations for academy training.[446]

On the evening of February 15, 1989, Scott met Maureen Brannick on a night out, and the two hit it off. Two years later, on Christmas Eve 1991, he asked Maureen to marry him. Their courtship would continue a few more years because of the state police class being put on hold. Scott wanted a secure job before settling down and then was offered a position with the Plainfield Police Department. While Gonzalez was in the Plainfield academy, Trooper Hanratty #4971 was killed and Scott attended the funeral. He was

156

impressed with the showing of law enforcement professionals from around the country.[447]

Gonzalez graduated from the local academy and began his tenure as a Plainfield police officer. Gonzalez learned to be a city cop. He was personable and mixed well with the citizens he served. However, six weeks into his tour as a local police officer, the state police beckoned. His marriage was put on hold.[448]

Gonzalez began training as a member of the 113th class in August 1992. Sadly, while in the academy, his grandmother passed away. Scott had hoped that she would see him become a trooper. The academy had not been easy on Scott. During this time he developed a painful ankle injury that had to be taped up before each day's physical training. Despite the pain of his injury, Scott endured. At night, he would soak his feet in buckets of ice to help keep the swelling down. On January 15, 1993, Scott Gonzalez graduated and was assigned badge #5059.[449]

Trooper Scott Gonzalez reported to work, donning the impressive uniform that he had so long wished to wear. Scott wasn't a big man; he stood only five feet, eight inches tall. Nonetheless, the brown-haired, hazel-eyed trooper had a stocky build and wore the uniform well. During his nearly five years in the outfit, Scott Gonzalez became a good trooper—fair, compassionate and unafraid of the dangers that lurk over the shoulder of each trooper. Scott was an avid reader of police survival techniques and became proficient with his handgun. Moreover, he "attended several classes on drug intervention" and other rated topics to enhance his performance as a road trooper. Gonzalez's tenure with the organization was spent in Troop B.[450]

In October 1993, Scott and Maureen purchased a house in Hampton, which is in Hunterdon County. On March 24, 1994, the couple were married in a ceremony in the Inglemoor Nursing Home in Livingston, New Jersey, in order for Maureen's mother, an inpatient, to witness the service. It was the highlight of the month for the residents there, and a small celebration was held.[451]

Throughout his life, Gonzalez was an outdoorsman who enjoyed "fishing and hunting." On the weekends, he enjoyed watching an occasional football or baseball game, but above all else, he liked to be outside. Always easy to get along with, he had a good sense of humor as well. "He liked to joke around," said Maureen. "He could be a "ball buster…but he had a good heart. He was good to his friends, and if you were good to him, he was good to you; otherwise, he would have nothing to do with you."[452]

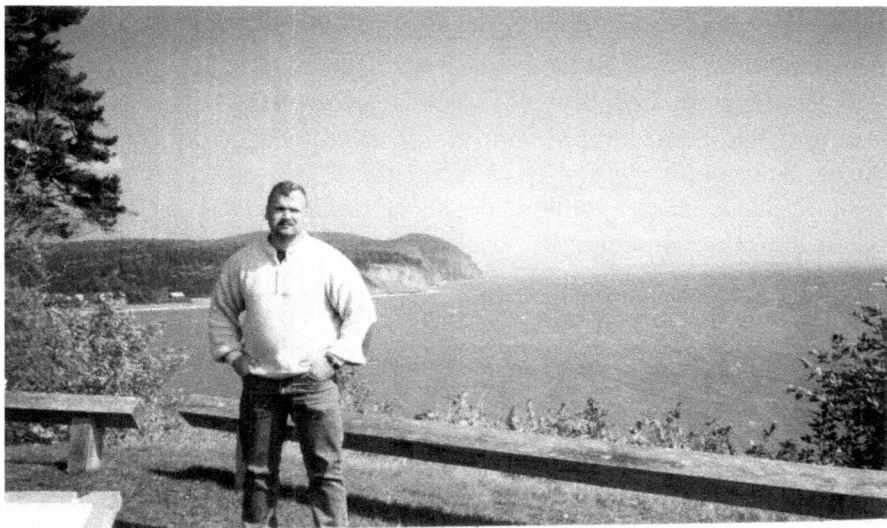

He loved the outdoors. *Courtesy of Maureen Gonzalez.*

Being in the construction business for all those years taught Scott to be a good craftsman. In their home, Scott laid down wood floors with crown molding, replaced all of his windows and did just about everything. Scott and Maureen enjoyed staying at home together and working on house projects. It was a nice quiet life for them and contrasted with the more exciting day-to-day work he did as a trooper. "He was proud," said Maureen "of wearing his uniform…it was his dream come true. Not many people can go to work and say they love their job."

Trooper Gonzalez had become quite a good trooper, attentive to malevolent behavior. A highlight of his career is the confiscation of eleven pounds of crack cocaine valued at $130,000. Gonzalez was a trooper through and through; if you called him a cop, he would say, "No, I'm a trooper." In June 1995, Scott attended the funeral of Trooper Marvin McCloud #4718. Less than a year later, in May 1996, he could be seen standing in formation for the funeral of Trooper Francis Bellaran #4429. With each mass he attended, Scott would take the mass card for the trooper and keep it in his hat. People would ask why he did that; he replied that "so that the trooper had not yet gone home, but was still on the road." Throughout his tenure with the organization, Gonzalez received fourteen letters of commendation and the coveted Yellow Ribbon (worn on uniform). However, the heroics he had performed in the past paled in comparison to his actions on Friday, October, 24, 1997.[453]

Digressing, momentarily, in late September or early October, Scott and Maureen went on an extended vacation, visiting Canada and then spending a considerable time together at home, with Scott renovating a bedroom and bath. A few days before returning to work, he and Maureen spent the day in Chester, New Jersey, window shopping. While there, he bought Maureen a single rose, which she put in a vase upon getting home. Although Gonzalez had a wonderful time off, he was looking forward to putting on his uniform again. Maureen once asked a hypothetical question to her husband: "What if you knew via a crystal ball that you were going to die on the job?" His response strikes to the core of the man he was: "I would go in to work, put on my best uniform, polish my brass, shine my leather and face it like a man, like the trooper I am. That is my job, and that is what I get paid to do. I'm not afraid." [454]

This brings us to the afternoon of October 24, 1997, with Maureen Gonzalez at home reaching into her refrigerator to grab candy that she had hidden from her husband, who was dieting. To her surprise, it was gone.

Funeral card.

She laughed and said, "Wait 'til he gets home." Meanwhile, Scott was following a pickup truck driven by Sammy Beatty Shipps, a deranged man whom Scott had dealt with before. Shipps had been arguing with his mother and had grabbed a loaded shotgun before running out of the house. Trooper Gonzalez spotted the truck and began providing location updates while trying to coordinate assistance from backup units. (This was trooper country, where there are no local cops nearby.) Backup for these troopers is often fifteen or maybe thirty minutes away; Gonzalez knew this, and so did Shipps.[455]

Scott's voice was calm, and he was collected during the entire

Maureen and Scott. *Courtesy of Maureen Gonzalez.*

period in which he followed Shipps. His last transmission came at 5:26 p.m.: "Be advised, the individual is not stopping." Shipps had driven down a private road that ended in a cul-de-sac, where Trooper Gonzalez decided to end his pursuit by blocking the egress out of the cul-de-sac. When he did so, Shipps drove straight into his troop car. The impact caused Scott's airbag to deploy, hitting him in the face. The front fenders on the Ford vehicle Gonzalez was driving were designed to bend, pinning the doors and preventing them from opening in a crash. However, this design feature prevented the trooper from being able to exit his car. In essence, he was trapped! With airbag soot filling the inside of the car, Gonzalez could barely see out of his windows. Then a shotgun blast came from Shipps, who fired at the state trooper. Gonzalez returned fire through his windshield, missing Shipps by inches. With the crazed gunman continuing to fire, Scott's handgun began to malfunction. Trapped with a malfunctioning weapon, and firing periodically, there were too many obstacles for Gonzalez to overcome. In the end, Shipps fired a blast that mortally wounded Gonzalez. The first person on the scene to help was Scott's sergeant. The supervisor had grabbed a shotgun from the closet and ran out of the station to help his trooper.[456]

After the funeral, Maureen noticed the rose Scott had bought her, went to empty the stale water and discovered the missing candy. It was as if Scott was still there, joking and teasing her. She had hidden it from him, and he had hidden it from her.[457]

A TRIBUTE

CHRISTOPHER S. SCALES #4575

Trooper Christopher Scales #4575.
Courtesy of the New Jersey State Police.

In law enforcement, tragedy can strike while doing the most mundane assignments. That's exactly what happened on Tuesday, December 3, 2002, at 11:15 a.m. Trooper Scales was conducting a seatbelt detail at Interchange 12 on the New Jersey Turnpike and had been standing near a tollbooth; as a tanker truck passed, Scales lost his footing and slipped off the concrete. The trooper fell under the rear wheels of a tanker truck as it was passing, and he was dragged to his death.[458]

Trooper Christopher Scales was forty years old and a father of three small children.[459]

ARMED ROBBERY

BERTRAM T. ZIMMERMAN III #5853

B ertram T. Zimmerman was an ambitious man who strove for personal betterment. Zimmerman, the surname of German descent, was the grandson of Bertram T. Zimmerman, who was a painter from Merchantville, New Jersey. There, he and his wife, Naomi (née May), lived a modest life in this small community. The couple had a son, Bertram T. Zimmerman II. When their son was a teenager, Naomi became stricken with cancer and died at forty-two. Helping the grieving widower cope with his wife's death was his sister-in-law, Claire The two clung to each other in this time of sorrow and eventually fell in love and married.[460]

Bertram spent long hours in his vocation, and the lead-based paint caused his early demise at fifty-five. Claire and her stepson were left devastated over the loss.[461]

As an adult, Bertram T. Zimmerman II met and fell in love with a Polish woman named Verna (née Przywara). Verna's father, John, was a truck driver, and her mother, Helen (née Supernak), worked for the RCA Corporation as a solderer. Bertram and Verna married in November 1967 and for a time lived with Claire until they could get established financially. Years later, records have the couple living in a townhouse at 25 Presidential Drive in Erial, New Jersey. There they would raise a family.[462]

The couple had three children together: Andrea, Jamie and Bertram T. Zimmerman III. Bertram was the middle of the three and was born on August 29, 1971.[463]

Trooper Bertram T. Zimmerman #5853. *Courtesy of Denise Zimmerman.*

All three children attended the Erial Grammar School in Sicklerville. Afterward, Bertram went to the Charles Lewis Middle School in Blackwood. Zimmerman loved sports and showed athleticism from an early age. With this interest, his parents enrolled him in the Pinehill Baseball Little League. Bert (as he was called) played a variety of positions, from pitcher to third baseman and eventually center fielder. Bert also enjoyed football and played on the high school team.[464]

In high school, Andrea says that her brother was the "life of the party." Everyone knew that he was a practical joker and enjoyed stirring things up at "get-togethers." High school was a joyous time for Bert, and he matured both intellectually and socially. Zimmerman was a solid "B" student throughout high school.[465]

By the time Zimmerman graduated, he stood six feet tall and had a long, slender build. He had light-brown hair, brown eyes and an olive skin complexion.[466]

On one particular day, Andrea was walking on a frozen pond, and the ice gave way. "I fell through the ice up to my waist," Andrea says. "Bert had to run and get a friend to help get me out." After rescuing his sister from the deadly cold water, Bert brought her home, dried her off and kept this as a secret from their parents. That was the kind of brother he was.[467]

As Zimmerman grew, he started collecting sports memorabilia and baseball cards. His father bought him Topps baseball cards for just about every occasion. Throughout the years, Bert acquired boxes on top of boxes of cards. He had an impressive collection of cards and sports merchandise. According to Andrea, her brother had enough cards to wallpaper a house. Zimmerman's favorite sports teams were the Philadelphia Phillies and the

Philadelphia Eagles. Living in south Jersey, the Zimmerman family attended many sporting events in historic Philadelphia. They even had season tickets to the Philadelphia Flyers hockey team.[468]

After high school, Bert set his sights on entering the field of law enforcement and took up criminal justice studies at the Gloucester County Community College. There Zimmerman continued playing baseball and was the team's center fielder. During the 1992 season, they won the championship, with Bert setting a team batting average record—a record still in existence today.[469]

Upon graduating junior college, he began taking classes at Rutgers University. Now twenty-two years old, Zimmerman applied as a special police officer for the Gloucester Township Police Department. He was appointed there and as a special police officer worked closely with seasoned officers. An opening came up for the Evesham Township Police Department in Burlington County, and Bert took the test, scoring high and ultimately becoming a sworn police officer there.[470]

Several years passed, and Zimmerman developed a reputation for writing a lot of tickets for the small community. Andrea laughs thinking about it: "He used to write so many tickets when he became a trooper they used to tell him to slow down." By July 1998, Bert had begun stopping at a local

His little puppy. *Courtesy of Denise Zimmerman.*

establishment called My Favorite Muffin for a bagel or muffin. As such, he became friendly with the store owner. On one occasion, he saw an attractive woman working there. He inquired who she was from the owner. The owner let this young woman, Denise Petrelli, know of the young officer's attraction. Denise was in graduate school and worked there on the weekends. She couldn't put a face on the mysterious man in uniform. The stars aligned one early morning for Zimmerman when Denise happened to be in the store. The two talked and exchanged phone numbers, with Bert calling her the very next day. Soon, they were in love and planning a life together. At this point in his life, Bert wanted to transition from being a local officer to being a New Jersey state trooper and had taken the examination for such.[471]

On March 14, 2001, there was a hard, cold chill in the air as the sun rose over the horizon only to be blocked by the thick cloud cover surrounding the Sea Girt, New Jersey area. On this day, Zimmerman put a new badge on his hat—a triangular one that bore #5853.[472]

Trooper Zimmerman had several assignments beginning at the Woodstown Station, with additional tours at Bellmawr and Tuckerton Stations before being stationed to the Troop A (a Tactical Patrol Unit). Although he had been a police officer and was now a trooper, he had been working side jobs as a construction worker for years. He had become an excellent carpenter. Bert liked working with his hands, and the extra money made it that much more rewarding. Bert Zimmerman was a goal-oriented person who worked to achieve his objectives.[473]

In April 2002, Bert purchased a two-story Cape Cod house at 24 Ohio Avenue in Blackwood New Jersey. The house was a quaint structure, with four bedrooms and an unfinished basement. Using his carpentry skills, Bert turned this space into a family room equipped with a bar built with his own hands.[474]

In August, while vacationing in the Bahamas, Bert asked Denise for her hand in marriage. The next twelve months saw the two preparing for their wedding. Bert and Denise had been a happy couple for over five years. In that time, they had become soul mates and spent many hours jet-skiing and entertaining their friends. They had endured a long-distance relationship twice—Denise's graduate school tenure and Bert's academy training. Moreover, Denise was with Bert through his municipal police days and the transition to a jersey trooper. Needless to say, as the years progressed, so did their love, so it is fitting that on Saturday, August 16, 2003, the two exchanged wedding vows at Saint Monica's Catholic Church in Philadelphia.[475]

Bert and Denise. *Courtesy of Denise Zimmerman.*

Their first Christmas together was a joyful one, with Bert giving Denise a Weimaraner puppy named Jayda. Bert told Denise that it was "to protect" her when she was home alone while he was working the night shift. Bert wanted his wife to feel safe. Another present Bert gave was a state police bib that proudly displaced the state police logo on it. He gave this to Andrea, who was expecting a child. (To this day, these presents are lasting tokens and links from Bert to his beloved wife and sister.)[476]

Always seeking to better himself, Bert had enrolled at Seton Hall University and was nearing the end of his studies for a graduate degree and looking forward to graduating in the spring. At work, rumors had it that Zimmerman was going to be selected for a position on the prestigious TEAMS (Tactical, Emergency and Mission Specialists) unit. TEAMS is the equivalent of Los Angeles Police Department's SWAT.[477]

In the early part of December, the first of a series of armed robberies took place at a Wawa convenience store in Pleasantville in the Atlantic County area. With each robbery, the suspect entered in a tactical position, wearing a ski mask and armed with a handgun. He would bound and gag his victims before leaving. In light of these robberies, a multi-agency task force was set up that included Zimmerman's TPU squad.[478]

Physical surveillance was conducted in early January 2004, but after a week, authorities became frustrated and postponed the operation. Then, on

January 22, 2004, the suspect hit again, and the task force was reestablished. Video cameras were set up in various Wawa stores that fed back to a state police command post. Moreover, surveillance teams were positioned in proximity to these selected Wawa stores, with Trooper Zimmerman being positioned at one of these locations.[479]

On Tuesday, February 3, 2004, Bert spent a portion of the day at his sister Andrea's home building a nursery for her expected child. Afterward, he stopped home and spent time with Denise. A trooper's job takes a toll on family life, but even so, Denise was fully supportive of her husband. That night, Denise was feeling under the weather and was going to bed early. Bert wished her well as she readied for bed and kissed her goodbye, saying that he would call later to see how she was feeling.[480]

Arriving at work, Trooper Zimmerman was given a surveillance post for the Wawa store located at Route 47 and Main Street in Dennis Township. True to his word, at 11:30 p.m. he called Denise. She heard the phone ring and laid in bed and listened as Bert left a voice message. She thought about picking up but still didn't feel well. She drifted back to sleep hearing his voice.[481]

Hours later, while sitting in his car, the state police radio sounded, killing the dead silence that filled air. The suspect had hit the Wawa store on Route 9 and Sea Isle Boulevard, just miles from Bert's location. The trooper activated his emergency lights and sped off.[482]

While racing to the crime scene, Zimmerman hit a patch of ice, lost control of his car, slid off the road and struck a utility pole. The impact caused the state cruiser to wrap around the pole like a horseshoe, eerily reminiscent of Trooper Bellaran's accident a few years prior. Needless to say, the outcome was just as tragic. Troopers held Zimmerman's hands, while rescuers frantically worked to extricate him from the car. In the end, Bert Zimmerman was not alone—he had fellow troopers by his side.[483]

At the funeral, Denise Zimmerman placed a stuffed dolphin pillow that she used to sleep with into Bert's coffin. (He used to tease her about it.) She had had the dolphin since she was a girl—it made her feel safe and warm and not alone. The grieving widow placed the stuffed animal beside her husband because she wanted him to know that she was always with him. Today, Bertram Zimmerman III sleeps in eternal rest with that pillow. For Denise, Bert had always told her that he would protect her. To this day, she feels that "he is her guardian angel from heaven."[484]

ANTAGONIST

MARC K. CASTELLANO #6397

In September 2009, the state police began a new chapter in its history. It was released from federal oversight that had stemmed from allegations of racial profiling during a 1999 shooting; spirits were high as troopers began a post–consent decree era. In February, the anniversary of Trooper Zimmerman's tragic death was memorialized, marking the second-longest period between line-of-duty deaths for the organization. A new generation of troopers had become tenured. This generation of troopers had not known what it was like to work without video cameras and federal scrutiny. This generation also had yet to witness a death of one of its own. Of this generation was a man named Marc Castellano.[485]

Marc Castellano was born on July 15, 1980, to Kenneth and Donna Castellano. The Castellanos had two children, Marc and Nicolas. After Nicolas's birth, they moved to White Road in Jackson, New Jersey.[486]

The Castellanos were active in their children's lives, and Donna was a class mother and "Team Mom," while Ken made sure that he attended his boys' sporting activities. The couple had a pool installed in the backyard, and Donna taught her boys to swim. Donna readily admits that she was a disciplinarian and was strict with Marc. Rules were set and expected to be abided by. Marc attended Saint Mary's Academy in Lakewood and then in fifth grade went to the Jackson Public School. Marc and Nicolas were close despite their four-year age difference. Marc was a good student, had many friends and enjoyed playing "football, baseball, basketball and riding his quad motorcycle."[487]

Trooper Marc Castellano #6397. *Courtesy of Donna (Castellano) Setaro.*

In high school, Marc was an "A" and "B" student; however, these grades didn't come easy and were due to hard work and good study habits. A passion of Marc's was collecting autographed pictures and baseball cards. He would hang the pictures on his wall and organize the cards in his closet. In school, Marc played as a linebacker on the football team. He met the woman of his dreams—Stephanie Carloni, who attended high school in the next town over—when he was sixteen. Marc and Stephanie were introduced by a mutual friend. At first, Stephanie didn't think that Marc was her type. He had long hair and she preferred short. Despite this, Marc's charm overcame this obstacle, and the two began dating.[488]

Marc had a job all during high school. He used to work at a gas station, and on weekends he rode his bicycle there, putting in hours on Saturday and Sunday. As Marc neared his seventeenth birthday, his parents bought him a car, which Marc would pay off in instalments. The white Hyundai Scoop was nearly paid off by the time Marc blew out his birthday candles. To instill a sense of worth, Marc was required to pay for his own gas and insurance. Donna says that when the keys to the Hyundai were turned over to him, they disconnected the AM/FM radio in his car out of fear that he wouldn't concentrate while driving. As overprotective as this was, Marc never gave them a hard time. He was a good kid and son. Once permission was granted for the system to be connected, Marc equipped his little Hyundai with a robust stereo system, which included a large boombox in the rear. He loved his car and transformed it into a super-looking sports car with mag wheels, neon lights and a muffler designed to make the vehicle sound like a muscle car. Stephanie laughed, saying, "Friends used to make fun of him over the car."[489]

Nicolas and Marc. *Courtesy of Donna (Castellano) Setaro.*

Free time saw Marc at Stephanie's, hanging out. Mario and Jean Carloni loved Marc, as did Stephanie's siblings. Jean said, "Marc was a wonderful kid…kind and gentle." She laughed at how much Marc "loved to eat." His favorite kind of food was Italian. Interestingly, with all his activities, Marc found time to learn the drums and even was part of a garage band.

Rock music was his favorite. This ambitious kid made the most of his time. Stephanie and him went to the movies or grabbed a bit to eat now and then. To support his hobbies, Marc continued to work and picked up a job at a print shop while still working pumping gas.[490]

By his senior year, Marc had grown, and his good looks were drawn from his Italian, German and Czechoslovakian ancestry. Standing six feet tall, with his crystal blue eyes, brown hair and muscular build, he was a senior attraction. Marc was also a man of conviction and character who had experienced a loving family who supported and encouraged him.[491]

After graduating high school, Marc enrolled at the Ocean County Community College and began studying public administration. The next two years witnessed the man working for a construction company thirty hours per week while maintaining a full college course load. To begin planning for his financial success, Marc set up a retirement account. His parents were footing his college tuition, so he was able to put money away for his future. Castellano graduated Ocean County at age twenty and enrolled at Rutgers University in New Brunswick. Marc's interest in a professional vocation was in the field of law enforcement because many from his family had been in that field. However, no one department stood out in his mind. It simply didn't matter as long as he became a police officer.[492]

After graduating Rutgers, Castellano began applying to various police departments in the state; in all, about ten departments had his application. The Toms River Police Department was going to hire Marc, but budget constraints put that prospect on hold.[493]

In 2004, Castellan became a candidate for the Manchester Police Department, and it looked as if he was going to enter that academy, but then the New Jersey State Police called. "I think in his mind he always wanted to be a trooper," said his mother. Marc knew that the trooper academy was not a walk in the park and began training as a member of the 136th class.[494]

Marc Castellano expected training to be brutal but didn't think that he would be hospitalized because of it. Marc became dehydrated, and doctors at first thought that he had kidney damage from it. Fortunately, this was not the case, and he was back in training after several tests.[495]

On Sunday, September 5, 2004, while home on weekend leave, Marc and Stephanie were wed in a service at Saint Veronica's Church in Howell. A reception followed at the Ramada Versailles Banquet Hall, with more than two hundred people attending. There would be no honeymoon, as Tuesday morning academy roll call beckoned. Two weeks later, family and friends gathered in Sea Girt to watch Marc receive badge #6397.[496]

Stephanie, Marc, Julianna and Vincent. *Courtesy of the Castellano family.*

The couple moved into a new home on Stratton Street in Howell. It was a beige ranch with three bedrooms, and together they renovated just about everything. The young couple enjoyed quiet nights together, going to Broadway shows, nights out in Atlantic City and hanging with friends and family. A hobby of Marc's was cooking, and through the years his father-in-law, Mario, taught him how to cook Italian cuisine using homemade pasta. Every Sunday, Marc and Stephanie went to her parents' house, where a large family spread was put out.[497]

In March 2006, Stephanie gave birth to their first child, daughter Julianna Marie. Two years later, a son, Vincent Marc, followed. "Marc took care of the kids," said Jean. He was a loving father and did more than his share of parenting. When he was home, he washed and fed his children and spent hours on end with them. When Marc came home from work, he headed toward the laundry room to change, and Julianna and Vincent waited eagerly at the door for "Daddy." They knew that once he was done changing, "it was Daddy time." At night, Marc read fairy tales to Julianna and sat in the rocking chair while feeding Vincent. "He did everything," said Stephanie. "He was genuine." Throughout his life, "Marc influenced many people...because of the high standards he set for himself and lived by."[498]

Stephanie and Marc shared many dreams and plans for their future. Marc had recently graduated from Fairleigh Dickinson University, obtaining a graduate degree. The two were building a life together until a sequence of events separated them from each other.[499]

On Sunday, June 6, 2010, a Camden County woman sent authorities on a bogus search in an attempt to cover up her own wrongdoings. While assisting in the search activities, Trooper Marc Castellano was struck and killed by a motorist. The inattentive driver was preoccupied with curiosity about the activities, rather than his driving, and struck and killed the high school sweetheart and father of two.[500] Inattentive drivers have plagued the outfit since its inception and remain a continuous thread sewn into the narrative of the state police. Ironically, the first appearance of this antagonist appeared in the narrative of Trooper Herman Gloor Jr. #240 on a quiet Sunday very much like this one.[501]

NOTES

SANDWICH AND A COFFEE
1. Wikipedia, "Camden, New Jersey," http://en.wikipedia.org/wiki/Camden,_New_Jersey.
2. Interview with Mazie Staas.
3. Ibid.
4. Ibid.
5. Ibid.
6. Ibid.
7. Ibid. Mazie Staas does not recall which brother it was. Sadly, the Staas brothers have passed away.
8. Ibid.; Former Troopers Association, *New Jersey State Police*; NJSP Personnel Order No. 134, August 30, 1954, NJSP division headquarters.
9. Interview with Mazie Staas; Former Troopers Association, *New Jersey State Police*; NJSP Personnel Order No. 134, August 30, 1954, NJSP division headquarters.
10. Interview with Mazie Staas; Former Troopers Association, *New Jersey State Police*; NJSP Personnel Order No. 134, August 30, 1954, NJSP division headquarters.
11. *Newark Sunday News*, December 3, 1961.
12. Interview with Mazie Staas.
13. Ibid.
14. Lieutenant J.J. Killeen #476 to Captain G.J. Martin, December 2, 1961.
15. NJSP Accident Report, December 2, 1961; NJSP Preliminary Report No. 4217, File 3, December 2, 1961; interview with Mazie Staas.
16. NJSP Accident Report, December 2, 1961; NJSP Preliminary Report No. 4217, File 3, December 2, 1961; interview with Mazie Staas.
17. NJSP Personnel Order No. 119, December 4, 1961.
18. Interview with Mazie Staas.
19. Ibid.
20. Ibid.

IN-SERVICE TRAINING

21. Interview with Carol Fiola (daughter), January 25, 2009.

22. Ibid.

23. Ibid.

24. Ibid.

25. Ibid.

26. Ibid.

27. Interview with Lieutenant Colonel Louis Taranto.

28. New Jersey State Police Personnel Order No. 1, January 10, 1955; New Jersey State Police, www.njsp.org.

29. NJSP Museum File for Raymond Fiola.

30. Ibid.; John O'Rourke, *Jersey Troopers: Sacrifice at the Altar of Public Service* (Charleston, SC: The History Press, 2010).

31. Interview with Carol Fiola; NJSP Museum File for Raymond Fiola.

32. O'Rourke, *Jersey Troopers*; NJSP Museum File for Raymond Fiola; Farmer's Almanac, http://www.almanac.com/weather.

33. Interview with Carol Fiola.

34. New Jersey State Police, www.njsp.org; interview with Lieutenant Colonel Louis Taranto.

35. Interview with Carol Fiola.

36. NJSP Personnel Order No. 121, October 22, 1959; interview with Carol Fiola.

37. Farmer's Almanac; NJSP Accident Report, February 19, 1962. Note: the location of this accident looks much the same as it did in 1962. The accident occurred a mile and a half west of CR-537 on CR-526. The section of CR-526 that meets CR-537 is known today as CR-571. At the time of the accident, CR-571 did not exist.

38. NJSP Accident Report, February 19, 1962; State of New Jersey Death Certificate for Raymond Philip Fiola, February 21, 1962.

39. NJSP Personnel Order No. 38, February 20, 1962.

A DAY LIKE NO OTHER

40. Interview with Jackie (DeFrino) Lynch.

41. Ibid.

42. Ibid.

43. Ibid.

44. Ibid.

45. Ibid.

46. Ibid.

47. O'Rourke, *Jersey Troopers*.

48. New Jersey State Police, www.njsp.org.

49. New Jersey Turnpike Authority Accident Report, June 11, 1962.

50. Interview with Jackie (DeFrino) Lynch.

51. Ibid.

52. NJSP Museum File for Milan Simcak; Survivors of the Triangle, www.survivorsofthetriangle.org.

53. NJSP Museum File for Milan Simcak; Survivors of the Triangle, www.survivorsofthetriangle.org.

54. O'Rourke, *Jersey Troopers*.

55. NJSP Museum File for Milan Simcak.

56. Ibid.; Survivors of the Triangle website; *Red Bank Register*, Wednesday, August 1, 1962.

57. NJSP Museum File for Arthur J. Abagnale Jr. Upon contacting the person who is believed to be the last family member, he did not want to participate in this book.

58. Ibid.

59. Ibid.

60. Ibid.

61. Ibid.

"SPIKE"

62. Interview with Patricia Lukis LeClair.

63. Wikipedia," Lithuania," http://en.wikipedia.org/wiki/Lithuania; House of Names, "Boyle Family Crest and Name History," http://www.houseofnames.com/boyle-family-crest; Wikipedia, "County Donegal," http://en.wikipedia.org/wiki/County_Donegal.

64. Interview with Patricia Lukis LeClair.

65. Ibid.

66. Ibid.

67. Ibid.

68. Ibid.

69. Ibid.

70. Ibid.

71. Ibid.

72. Ibid.

73. O'Rourke, *Jersey Troopers*.

74. Interview with Patricia Lukis LeClair.

75. Ibid.

76. Ibid.; *Bucks County Times*, May 4, 1966.

77. NJSP Personnel Order No. 48, June 1, 1965.

78. Interview with Patricia Lukis LeClair.

79. NJSP Formal Statement of Daniel Connors Kremens, taken May 4, 1966, at 7:05 a.m.

80. *State of New Jersey v. Daniel Kremens*, decided on July 5, 1966, citation number unavailable.

81. Ibid.

82. Harry Camisa and Jim Franklin, *Inside Out: Fifty Years Behind the Walls of New Jersey's Trenton Prison* (Hamburg, PA: Windsor Press and Publishing, 2008).

83. Interview with Patricia Lukis LeClair.

SPILLED LOAD

84. Interview with Robert Kavula, January 30, 2009.

85. Ibid.

86. Ibid.

87. Ibid.

88. Ibid.

89. Ibid.

90. Ibid.

91. Ibid.; interview with Sheila Kavula, January 26, 2009.

92. Interview with Robert Kavula; interview with Sheila Kavula.

93. Interview with Robert Kavula; interview with Sheila Kavula.

94. Interview with Sheila Kavula.

95. Ibid.

96. Ibid.

97. Ibid.

98. Interview with Sheila Kavula; interview with Robert Kavula; New Jersey State Police Personnel Information Form, February 13 (year unreadable); untitled New Jersey State Police document, January 21, 1963; New Jersey State Police Operations Instructions, June 24, 1963; J.J. Harris to Commanders, Troops A, B, C, Operations Officer and Academy Commandant, June 24, 1964.

99. Interview with Sheila Kavula; interview with Robert Kavula; New Jersey State Police Personnel Information Form, February 13 (year unreadable); untitled New Jersey State Police document, January 21, 1963; New Jersey State Police Operations Instructions, June 24, 1963; J.J. Harris to Commanders, Troops A, B, C, Operations Officer and Academy Commandant, June 24, 1964.

100. Interview with Sheila Kavula.

101. Ibid.; interview with Robert Kavula.

102. The Newark Station during Kavula's tour there was located in what now is the administrative building at Interchange 14.

103. Interview with Robert Kavula; author's knowledge of what troopers call the turnpike.

104. Interview with Sheila Kavula; Leo Coakley, *Jersey Troopers* (Piscataway, NJ: Rutgers University Press, 1971); Wikipedia, "Robert F. Kennedy," http://en.wikipedia.org/wiki/Robert_F._Kennedy; Wikipedia, "Martin Luther King Jr.," http://en.wikipedia.org/wiki/Martin_Luther_King,_Jr.

105. Interview with Sheila Kavula.

106. Ibid.

107. Ibid.; NJSP Accident Report, September 19, 1968. Note: The present-day driveway leading into the administration building parking lot at Interchange 13 was the location of the temporary ramp to the Goathals Bridge in 1968.

108. NJSP Accident Report, September 19, 1968; Detective F.J. Cordes #1527 to Major V. Galassi, September 30, 1968.

109. Interview with Sheila Kavula; interview with Robert Kavula.

110. Interview with Sheila Kavula; interview with Robert Kavula; NJSP Museum File for Thomas Kavula.

STRUCK DOWN BY A DRUNK

111. Interview with Joann Prato.

112. Ibid.

113. Ibid.

114. Ibid.

115. Ibid.
116. Ibid.
117. Ibid.
118. Ibid.
119. Ibid.; New Jersey State Police, www.njsp.org.
120. Interview with Joann Prato; New Jersey State Police, www.njsp.org.
121. Interview with Joann Prato; NJSP Museum File for Robert Prato.
122. Interview with Joann Prato; NJSP Museum File for Robert Prato.
123. Interview with Joann Prato.
124. Ibid.
125. Ibid.
126. Ibid.; NJSP Museum File for Robert Prato.
127. Interview with Joann Prato; NJSP Museum File for Robert Prato.
128. Ibid.
129. Joann Prato to John O'Rourke, November 16, 2011.

Train Crossing
130. Interview with Cheryl (Moesta) Storck.
131. Ibid.
132. Ibid.
133. Ibid.
134. Ibid.
135. Ibid.; Jana Perskie to John E. O'Rourke, March 21, 2011.
136. Interview with Cheryl (Moesta) Storck.
137. Ibid.
138. Ibid.
139. Ibid.
140. Ibid.
141. Ibid.
142. Ibid.
143. NJSP Personnel Order No. 29, February 11, 1970; NJSP Personnel Order No. 66, April 30, 1970.
144. Staff Sergeant H.F. Theurer to Captain J.A. Carpani, November 19, 1970.
145. Ibid.; Lieutenant J.R. Brennan to Captain J.A. Carpani, November 30, 1970.
146. Staff Sergeant H.F. Theurer to Captain J.A. Carpani, November 19, 1970; Lieutenant J.R. Brennan to Captain J.A. Carpani, November 30, 1970.
147. NJSP, *The Triangle* 3, no. 9 (November 1970).

Call Me Rennie
148. Wikipedia, "Birthright Citizenship in the United States," http://en.wikipedia.org/wiki/Birthright_citizenship_in_the_United_States#CITEREFMeese2005; interview with Lynne (Segeren) Freedman.
149. Interview with Lynne (Segeren) Freedman.
150. Ibid.
151. Ibid.
152. Ibid.

153. Ibid.
154. Ibid.
155. Ibid.
156. Ibid.
157. Ibid.
158. Ibid.
159. Ibid.
160. Ibid.
161. Ibid.
162. Ibid.
163. Ibid.; NJSP Personnel Information Form for Marienus Segeren, February 7, 1968.
164. Author's perspective.
165. Former Troopers Association, *New Jersey State Police*; interview with Lynne (Segeren) Freedman.
166. NJSP Personnel Order No. 11, February 3, 1969; NJSP Biography Document of Marienus Segeren, n.d.
167. Interview with Lynne (Segeren) Freedman.
168. Ibid.
169. Ibid.; NJSP Special Report; Lieutenant E.E. Doremus to Captain W.J. Wildes, July 30, 1971.
170. Interview with Lynne (Segeren) Freedman; NJSP Special Report; Lieutenant E.E. Doremus to Captain W.J. Wildes, July 30, 1971.
171. Interview with Lynne (Segeren) Freedman; NJSP Special Report; Lieutenant E.E. Doremus to Captain W.J. Wildes, July 30, 1971; author's perspective.
172. NJSP Accident Report A1671141A, July 25, 1971.
173. Interview with Lynne (Segeren) Freedman.
174. Ibid.

It Can't Happen to Him!

175. NJSP Museum File for Robert J. Merenda; interview with Ronald Perozzi.
176. Interview with Ronald Perozzi.
177. NJSP Applicant Investigation Report of Robert J. Merenda, September 18, 1968.
178. Ibid.; interview with Ronald Perozzi.
179. NJSP Applicant Investigation Report of Robert J. Merenda, September 18, 1968; interview with Ronald Perozzi.
180. NJSP Applicant Investigation Report of Robert J. Merenda, September 18, 1968; interview with Ronald Perozzi.
181. NJSP Applicant Investigation Report of Robert J. Merenda, September 18, 1968; interview with Ronald Perozzi.
182. NJSP Applicant Investigation Report of Robert J. Merenda, September 18, 1968; interview with Ronald Perozzi.
183. NJSP Museum File for Robert J. Merenda; Coakley, *Jersey Troopers*.
184. NJSP Museum File for Robert J. Merenda; Coakley, *Jersey Troopers*; Cumberland County, New Jersey, http://www.co.cumberland.nj.us/content/163/241/591.aspx; Wikipedia, "Charles K. Landis," http://en.wikipedia.org/wiki/Charles_K._Landis.
185. NJSP Museum File for Robert J. Merenda; Wikipedia, "Charles K. Landis."
186. Interview with James Principe.

187. Interview with Ronald Perozzi.

188. Ibid.; Pro Football Hall of Fame, www.profootballhof.com/history/stats/thanksgiving.aspx.

189. O'Rourke, *Jersey Troopers*.

190. NJSP Preliminary Report No. 4980, File 3, November 29, 1971.

191. Interview with Ronald Perozzi; interview with James Principe.

SHOOTOUT WITH THE BLACK LIBERATION ARMY

192. Interview with Ronald Foster #2240.

193. Ibid.

194. Ibid.; Werner Foerster Certificate of Death; Wikipedia, "Assata Shakur," http://en.wikipedia.org/wiki/Assata_Shakur#cite_note-36.

195. Interview with Ronald Foster #2240; Werner Foerster Certificate of Death; Wikipedia, "Assata Shakur," http://en.wikipedia.org/wiki/Assata_Shakur#cite_note-36.

196. Interview with Ronald Foster #2240; Werner Foerster Certificate of Death.

197. NJSP Investigative Report H207396, May 14, 1973.

198. New Jersey State Police, www.njsp.org; *Lincoln Star*, March 26, 1977; *Post-Standard*, March 26, 1977.

199. Contact was made with Rosa Foerster by this author. Unfortunately, she didn't want to speak about her husband and advised that her son wouldn't want to speak on the subject either.

200. Survivors of the Triangle website.

201. NJSP Museum File for Werner Foerster.

202. Ibid.

203. NJSP Personnel Order No. 62, April 20, 1970; NJSP Personnel Order No. 109, July 6, 1970.

204. NJSP Museum File for Werner Foerster.

205. Ibid.

DETECTIVE

206. Interview with Ingrid Dawson.

207. Ibid.; Wikipedia, "Hamilton Square, New Jersey," http://en.wikipedia.org/wiki/Hamilton_Square,_New_Jersey.

208. NJSP Museum File for Thomas A. Dawson; interview with Ingrid Dawson.

209. Interview with Ingrid Dawson.

210. Ibid.

211. Ibid.; NJSP Museum File for Thomas A. Dawson.

212. Interview with Ingrid Dawson; NJSP Museum File for Thomas A. Dawson.

213. Interview with Ingrid Dawson; NJSP Museum File for Thomas A. Dawson.

214. Interview with Ingrid Dawson; NJSP Museum File for Thomas A. Dawson.

215. Interview with Ingrid Dawson; NJSP Museum File for Thomas A. Dawson.

216. Interview with Ingrid Dawson; NJSP Alert Report No. 448, File 3, August 14, 1973; NJSP Museum File for Thomas A. Dawson.

217. Interview with Ingrid Dawson.

Trooper of the Year

218. Statement by John Delesio, no date.

219. Interview with Grace, Debbie and Diane Lamonaco; interview with Donna Lamonaco, June 2, 2009.

220. Interview with Grace, Debbie and Diane Lamonaco; interview with Donna Lamonaco, June 2, 2009.

221. Interview with Grace, Debbie and Diane Lamonaco; interview with Donna Lamonaco, June 2, 2009.

222. Interview with Grace, Debbie and Diane Lamonaco; interview with Donna Lamonaco, June 2, 2009.

223. Interview with Grace, Debbie and Diane Lamonaco; interview with Donna Lamonaco, June 2, 2009.

224. Interview with Grace, Debbie and Diane Lamonaco; interview with Donna Lamonaco, June 2, 2009.

225. Interview with Grace, Debbie and Diane Lamonaco; interview with Donna Lamonaco, June 2, 2009.

226. Interview with Grace, Debbie and Diane Lamonaco; interview with Donna Lamonaco, June 2, 2009.

227. Interview with Grace, Debbie and Diane Lamonaco; interview with Donna Lamonaco, June 2, 2009.

228. Interview with Grace, Debbie and Diane Lamonaco; interview with Donna Lamonaco, June 2, 2009.

229. Military Vet Shop, "A Summary History of the 3rd Marine Division" http://www.militaryvetshop.com/History/3rdMarDiv.html.

230. Former Troopers Association, *New Jersey State Police*.

231. Interview with Donna Lamonaco, June 2, 2009.

232. Ibid.

233. Ibid.

234. Ibid.

235. Ibid.

236. Ibid.

237. Ibid.

238. Ibid.

239. Ibid.

240. Interview with Nona, Dorothy, Brian and Noreen McCarthy.

241. NJSP Museum File for Philip Lamonaco.

242. Interview with Donna Lamonaco, June 2, 2009.

243. Ibid.; New Jersey Lawman, "Joanne Chesimard," http://www.njlawman.com/Feature%20Pieces/Joanne%20Chesimard.htm.

244. Interview with Donna Lamonaco.

245. Ibid.

246. Ibid.

247. Ibid.

248. NJSP Museum File for Philip Lamonaco.

249. Ibid.

250. Interview with Donna Lamonaco.

251. NJSP Museum File for Philip Lamonaco.

The Black Dragon

252. Interview with Nona (McCarthy) Dalrymple, Dorothy and Brian McCarthy and Noreen (McCarthy) Cryan.

253. O'Rourke, *Jersey Troopers*.

254. Interview with Nona (McCarthy) Dalrymple, Dorothy and Brian McCarthy and Noreen (McCarthy) Cryan; Nona (McCarthy) Dalrymple to John O'Rourke, November 19, 2011.

255. Interview with Nona (McCarthy) Dalrymple, Dorothy and Brian McCarthy and Noreen (McCarthy) Cryan; Nona (McCarthy) Dalrymple to John O'Rourke, November 19, 2011.

256. Interview with Nona (McCarthy) Dalrymple, Dorothy and Brian McCarthy and Noreen (McCarthy) Cryan; Nona (McCarthy) Dalrymple to John O'Rourke, November 19, 2011.

257. Interview with Nona (McCarthy) Dalrymple, Dorothy and Brian McCarthy and Noreen (McCarthy) Cryan; Nona (McCarthy) Dalrymple to John O'Rourke, November 19, 2011.

258. Interview with Nona (McCarthy) Dalrymple, Dorothy and Brian McCarthy and Noreen (McCarthy) Cryan; Nona (McCarthy) Dalrymple to John O'Rourke, November 19, 2011.

259. Interview with Nona (McCarthy) Dalrymple, Dorothy and Brian McCarthy and Noreen (McCarthy) Cryan; Nona (McCarthy) Dalrymple to John O'Rourke, November 19, 2011.

260. Interview with Nona (McCarthy) Dalrymple, Dorothy and Brian McCarthy and Noreen (McCarthy) Cryan; Nona (McCarthy) Dalrymple to John O'Rourke, November 19, 2011.

261. Interview with Nona (McCarthy) Dalrymple, Dorothy and Brian McCarthy and Noreen (McCarthy) Cryan; Nona (McCarthy) Dalrymple to John O'Rourke, November 19, 2011.

262. Interview with Nona (McCarthy) Dalrymple, Dorothy and Brian McCarthy and Noreen (McCarthy) Cryan; Nona (McCarthy) Dalrymple to John O'Rourke, November 19, 2011.

263. Interview with Nona (McCarthy) Dalrymple, Dorothy and Brian McCarthy and Noreen (McCarthy) Cryan; Nona (McCarthy) Dalrymple to John O'Rourke, November 19, 2011.

264. Interview with Nona (McCarthy) Dalrymple, Dorothy and Brian McCarthy and Noreen (McCarthy) Cryan; Nona (McCarthy) Dalrymple to John O'Rourke, November 19, 2011; NJSP Museum File for John McCarthy; O'Rourke, *Jersey Trooper*.

265. Interview with Nona (McCarthy) Dalrymple, Dorothy and Brian McCarthy and Noreen (McCarthy) Cryan; New Jersey State Police Personnel Information Form, January 30, 1978.

266. Author's personal account of ceremony, as he was at the graduation; NJSP Museum File for John McCarthy.

267. Interview with Nona (McCarthy) Dalrymple, Dorothy and Brian McCarthy and Noreen (McCarthy) Cryan.

268. Ibid.; NJSP Museum File for John P. McCarthy.

269. Interview with Nona (McCarthy) Dalrymple, Dorothy and Brian McCarthy and Noreen (McCarthy) Cryan; NJSP Museum File for John P. McCarthy; O'Rourke, *Jersey Troopers*.

270. Interview with Nona (McCarthy) Dalrymple, Dorothy and Brian McCarthy and Noreen (McCarthy) Cryan; NJSP Museum File for John P. McCarthy; O'Rourke, *Jersey Troopers*.

271. NJSP Museum File for John McCarthy.

272. Interview with Nona (McCarthy) Dalrymple, Dorothy and Brian McCarthy and Noreen (McCarthy) Cryan.

273. Ibid.

274. Ibid.

275. Ibid.

276. NJSP Museum File for John P. McCarthy.

ONE HELL OF A STRONG MAN

277. Interview with Colonel Clinton Pagano.

278. Frank Wertheim, *The Papers of Will Rogers* (Norman: University of Oklahoma Press, 2000); Circus History, "Bandwagon," http://www.circushistory.org/Bandwagon/bw-1971Mar.htm.

279. Interview with Colonel Clinton Pagano.

280. Ibid.

281. Ibid.

282. Ibid.

283. Ibid.

284. Ibid.

285. Ibid.

286. Ibid.

287. Ibid.

288. Ibid.

289. Ibid.

290. Ibid.

291. Ibid.

292. Ibid.; Gerald Tomilinson, *Murdered in Jersey* (New Brunswick, NJ: Rutgers University Press, 1994).

293. Tomilinson, *Murdered in Jersey*.

294. Ibid.; interview with Colonel Clinton Pagano.

295. Interview with Colonel Clinton Pagano.

296. Ibid.

297. Ibid.

298. Ibid.

299. Former Troopers Association, *New Jersey State Police*.

300. Interview with Colonel Clinton Pagano; Tomilinson, *Murdered in Jersey*.

301. Interview with Colonel Clinton Pagano.

302. NJSP, *The Triangle* 3, no. 5 (1983).

303. NJSP Museum File for Lester Pagano.

304. Interview with Colonel Clinton Pagano.

305. Ibid.

306. Captain R.L. Maralla to Colonel Clinton L. Pagano, Superintendent, August 9, 1983; NJSP Teletype No. 1026, File 3, July 19, 1983.
307. NJSP, *The Triangle* 3, no. 5 (1983).

ALWAYS A SMILE ON HIS FACE
308. Interview with Rita Errickson.
309. Ibid.
310. NJSP Museum File for Edward R. Errickson.
311. Ibid.
312. NJSP Teletype No. 203, File 14, January 26, 1984.

TROOPER DOWN
313. Jennie Negron-Bethea, *In Loving Memory of New Jersey State Trooper Carlos M. Negron* (N.p.: Llumina Press, 2003).
314. Ibid.
315. Ibid.
316. Ibid.
317. Ibid.
318. Ibid.
319. Ibid.
320. NJSP Personnel Order No. 145, July 15, 1983.
321. NJSP Teletype No. 479, File 3, May 7, 1984; *Trenton Times*, May 8, 1984.
322. NJSP Preliminary Report No. 476, File 3, May 7, 1984.

A WEDDING AND A FUNERAL
323. Interview with Christopher Carroll; NJSP Museum File for William L. Carroll Jr.
324. Interview with Christopher Carroll; NJSP Museum File for William L. Carroll Jr.
325. Interview with Christopher Carroll; NJSP Museum File for William L. Carroll Jr.
326. William L. Carroll Jr. NJSP Applicant Investigation.
327. Interview with Christopher Carroll.
328. Ibid.; NJSP Personnel Order No. 18, January 26, 1979; author's knowledge of state police graduations during this period.
329. NJSP Personnel Order No. 118, June 21, 1979.
330. Interview with Christopher Carroll.
331. Interview with Michelle Carroll.
332. NJSP Personnel Order No. 255, October 29, 1982.
333. NJSP Museum File for William L. Carroll Jr.; O'Rourke, *Jersey Troopers*; New Jersey State Police, www.njsp.org.
334. Interview with Michelle Carroll.
335. Ibid.
336. NJSP Accident Report D01084592A, July 12, 1984.
337. Ibid.
338. Ibid.; Autopsy Report of William Caroll Jr., July 13, 1984.
339. Interview with Michelle Carroll.

RAID

340. Interview with Peggie Mallen.
341. Ibid.
342. Ibid.
343. Ibid.
344. Ibid.
345. Ibid.
346. Ibid.
347. Ibid.
348. Ibid.
349. Ibid.
350. Ibid.
351. Ibid.
352. Ibid.
353. Ibid.
354. Ibid.
355. NJSP Museum File for Albert J. Mallen Sr.
356. Interview with Peggie Mallen; O'Rourke, *Jersey Troopers*.
357. Interview with Peggie Mallen; O'Rourke, *Jersey Troopers*.
358. Interview with Peggie Mallen; O'Rourke, *Jersey Troopers*.
359. NJSP Museum File for Albert J. Mallen Sr.; interview with Peggie Mallen.
360. Interview with Peggie Mallen.
361. Ibid.
362. *Star-Ledger*, August 30, 1985; *Daily Intelligencer*, Friday, August 30, 1985.
363. *Star-Ledger*, August 30, 1985; *Daily Intelligencer*, Friday, August 30, 1985; NJSP Museum File for Albert J. Mallen Sr.
364. *Star-Ledger*, August 30, 1985; *Daily Intelligencer*, Friday, August 30, 1985; NJSP Museum File for Albert J. Mallen Sr.
365. Interview with Peggie Mallen.
366. NJSP Museum File for Albert J. Mallen Sr.; NJSP, *The Triangle* (no date).

EVEN THE SIMPLEST CALL CAN BE PERILOUS

367. NJSP Museum File for Theodore J. Moos.
368. Interview with Nancy Moos.
369. Ibid.
370. Ibid.
371. Ibid.
372. Ibid.
373. Ibid.
374. Ibid.
375. Ibid.
376. Ibid.; O'Rourke, *Jersey Troopers*.
377. NJSP Museum File for Theodore J. Moos.
378. Interview with Nancy Moos.
379. Ibid.

380. Ibid.
381. Ibid.
382. Ibid.

Directions, Please?
383. Interview with Nancy Hanratty.
384. Ibid.
385. Ibid.
386. Ibid.
387. Ibid.
388. Ibid.
389. Ibid.
390. Ibid.
391. Ibid.
392. Interview with Trooper James Dobak #4287.
393. Interview with Nancy Hanratty.
394. Ibid.
395. O'Rourke, *Jersey Troopers*.
396. Interview with Nancy Hanratty.
397. NJSP Teletype Message No. 228, File 3, April 3, 1992.
398. Ibid.
399. Ibid.; *Star-Ledger*, Friday, April 3, 1992.
400. Interview with Nancy Hanratty.
401. *Star-Ledger*, Friday, April 3, 1992.
402. Interview with Nancy Hanratty.
403. *Star-Ledger*, Wednesday, March 17, 1993.

"A Smile that Could Light Up the World"
404. *Courier-Post*, Sunday, June 11, 1995.
405. *Courier-Post*, Saturday, June 10, 1995.
406. Ibid.
407. NJSP Museum File for Marvin R. McCloud.
408. *Courier-Post*, Sunday, June 11, 1995.
409. Ibid.
410. Ibid.
411. Ibid.
412. Ibid.
413. NJSP Museum File for Marvin R. McCloud.
414. *Courier-Post*, Sunday, June 11, 1995.
415. Ibid.
416. Ibid.

High-Speed Pursuit
417. Wikipedia, "Red Bank, New Jersey," http://en.wikipedia.org/wiki/Red_Bank,_New_Jersey#cite_ref-Story_5-0.

418. O'Rourke, *Jersey Troopers*.
419. Interview with Carol Bellaran; interview with Francis Bellaran.
420. Interview with Carol Bellaran; interview with Francis Bellaran.
421. Interview with Carol Bellaran; interview with Francis Bellaran.
422. Interview with Carol Bellaran; interview with Francis Bellaran.
423. Interview with Judy Bellaran.
424. Interview with Carol Bellaran; interview with Judy Bellaran.
425. Interview with Judy Bellaran.
426. Interview with Carol Bellaran; interview with Francis Bellaran; interview with Judy Bellaran.
427. NJSP Museum File for Francis J. Bellaran.
428. Interview with Carol Bellaran.
429. Author's personal knowledge.
430. Interview with Carol Bellaran; interview with Francis Bellaran; interview with Judy Bellaran.
431. Interview with Judy Bellaran.
432. Ibid.
433. Ibid.
434. Ibid.
435. Ibid.
436. NJSP Museum File for Frank Bellaran.
437. Ibid.
438. Ibid.
439. *Asbury Park Press*, May 24, 1996; *Star-Ledger*, Friday, May 24, 1996.
440. *Asbury Park Press*, May 24, 1996.
441. *Asbury Park Press*, October 18, 1997.

TRAPPED

442. Interview with Maureen Gonzalez.
443. Ibid.
444. Ibid.
445. Ibid.
446. Ibid.
447. Ibid.
448. Ibid.
449. Ibid.; Former Troopers Association, *New Jersey State Police*.
450. Interview with Maureen Gonzalez; Maureen Gonzalez to John O'Rourke, November 15, 2011.
451. Interview with Maureen Gonzalez; Maureen Gonzalez to John O'Rourke, November 15, 2011.
452. Interview with Maureen Gonzalez; Maureen Gonzalez to John O'Rourke, November 15, 2011.
453. Interview with Maureen Gonzalez; Maureen Gonzalez to John O'Rourke, November 15, 2011.
454. Interview with Maureen Gonzalez; Maureen Gonzalez to John O'Rourke, November 15, 2011.
455. NJSP Museum File for Scott M. Gonzalez.

456. Ibid.; author's own knowledge based on listening to audio transmissions.

457. Interview with Maureen Gonzalez.

A Tribute

458. NJSP Museum File for Christopher Scales.

459. Due to family conflicts the author was unable to include a full narrative on Christopher Scales.

Armed Robbery

460. Interview with Andrea Zimmerman (sister).

461. Ibid.

462. Ibid.

463. NJSP Museum File for Bertram T. Zimmerman.

464. Ibid.

465. Ibid.

466. Ibid.

467. Ibid.

468. Ibid.

469. Ibid.

470. Ibid.

471. Interview with Andrea Zimmerman (sister); interview with Denise Zimmerman; NJSP Museum File for Bertram Zimmerman III.

472. Interview with Andrea Zimmerman (sister); interview with Denise Zimmerman; NJSP Museum File for Bertram Zimmerman III.

473. Interview with Andrea Zimmerman (sister); interview with Denise Zimmerman; NJSP Museum File for Bertram Zimmerman III.

474. Interview with Denise Zimmerman.

475. Ibid.

476. Interview with Andrea Zimmerman (sister); interview with Denise Zimmerman.

477. Interview with Denise Zimmerman.

478. NJSP Museum File for Bertram Zimmerman III.

479. Ibid.

480. Interview with Denise Zimmerman.

481. Ibid.

482. NJSP Museum File for Bertram Zimmerman III.

483. Interview with Denise Zimmerman.

484. Ibid.

Antagonist

485. Author's own personal knowledge and perspective.

486. Interview with Donna (Castellano) Setaro.

487. Ibid.; Donna (Castellano) Setaro to John O'Rourke, December 4, 2011.

488. Interview with Donna (Castellano) Setaro; Donna (Castellano) Setaro to John O'Rourke, December 4, 2011; interview with Stephanie Castellano.

489. Interview with Donna (Castellano) Setaro; Donna (Castellano) Setaro to John O'Rourke, December 4, 2011; interview with Stephanie Castellano.

490. Interview with Donna (Castellano) Setaro; Donna (Castellano) Setaro to John O'Rourke, December 4, 2011; interview with Stephanie Castellano.

491. Interview with Donna (Castellano) Setaro; Donna (Castellano) Setaro to John O'Rourke, December 4, 2011; interview with Stephanie Castellano.

492. Interview with Donna (Castellano) Setaro; Donna (Castellano) Setaro to John O'Rourke, December 4, 2011; interview with Stephanie Castellano.

493. Interview with Donna (Castellano) Setaro; Donna (Castellano) Setaro to John O'Rourke, December 4, 2011; interview with Stephanie Castellano.

494. Interview with Donna (Castellano) Setaro; Donna (Castellano) Setaro to John O'Rourke, December 4, 2011; interview with Stephanie Castellano.

495. Interview with Donna (Castellano) Setaro; Donna (Castellano) Setaro to John O'Rourke, December 4, 2011; interview with Stephanie Castellano.

496. Interview with Stephanie Castellano; NJSP Museum File for Marc Castellano.

497. Interview with Stephanie Castellano; NJSP Museum File for Marc Castellano.

498. Interview with Stephanie Castellano; NJSP Museum File for Marc Castellano; Donna (Castellano) Setaro to John O'Rourke, December 4, 2011.

499. Interview with Stephanie Castellano; NJSP Museum File for Marc Castellano; Donna (Castellano) Setaro to John O'Rourke, December 4, 2011.

500. *Star-Ledger*, Monday, June 7, 2010.

501. O'Rourke, *Jersey Troopers*.

ABOUT THE AUTHOR

John E. O'Rourke was born in Pequannock, New Jersey, and was raised in the Passaic County town of Wanaque. O'Rourke's education includes a bachelor of science degree from Thomas Edison State College and a master of arts degree from Seton Hall University. He was a New Jersey state trooper for nearly twenty-six years and has extensive experience in security and leadership. O'Rourke is board certified in security management from ASIS International and heads its Crime and Loss Prevention Council. Presently, O'Rourke is the security manager for Montclair Golf Club in New Jersey and is an independent security consultant.

Visit us at
www.historypress.net